THE PARABLES OF JESUS

J. DWIGHT PENTECOST

**Academie
Books** Grand Rapids,
Michigan
Zondervan Publishing House

THE PARABLES OF JESUS
Copyright © 1982 by The Zondervan Corporation
Grand Rapids, Michigan

ACADEMIE BOOKS is an imprint of Zondervan
Publishing House, 1415 Lake Drive, S.E.,
Grand Rapids, Michigan 49506

Library of Congress Cataloging in Publication Data

Pentecost, J. Dwight.
  The parables of Jesus.

  1. Jesus Christ—Parables.   I. Title.
BT375.2.P46   226'.806   82-7000
ISBN 0-310-30961-1   AACR2

All rights reserved. No part of this publication may be reproduced,
stored in a retrieval system, or transmitted in any form or by any
means—electronic, mechanical, photocopy, recording, or any other—
except for brief quotations in printed reviews, without the prior
permission of the publisher.

Edited by John Danilson and Ben Chapman

Printed in the United States of America

87 88 89 90 91 92 93 / EP / 14 13 12 11 10 9 8 7

TABLE OF CONTENTS

PREFACE

The parables of Jesus have long challenged expositors and stimulated preachers, for in their simple form the deepest truths have been revealed. But the very simplicity has been a deceptive snare to the interpreter. An examination of writings shows that instead of considering the contexts in which the parables arise and the background against which they were spoken, many have pressed the parables to present truths that were in their minds as interpreters, but did not originate in the text itself. Some pulpiteers have used an allegorical method of interpretation to impress congregations with their abilities to discover truth in the words of Christ hitherto undiscovered. It is often overlooked that the primary purpose of the parables was to instruct those to whom the parables were originally spoken.

In this brief work an attempt will be made, through a study of the contexts in which the parables were spoken and the background against which they were delivered, to discover and present the essential truths the Lord sought to convey. Since the parables were primarily designed to instruct, emphasis will be placed on the teaching rather than the application. Proper application can be made only if based on proper interpretation. The concern of the author is to interpret the Lord's words to discover His instruction.

It is the author's desire that the reader be led into a clearer understanding of the truth contained in the parables and into a deeper love of the One of whom it was said, "No one ever spoke the way this man does" (John 7:46). In this work direct Scripture quotations are from the New International Version.

INTRODUCTION

Figures of speech are a part of every language. They embellish and enrich the language. How prosaic the Song of Solomon would be if the lovers did not express their love in the rich figures they used! But figures do more than adorn the language. They are the means by which abstract ideas are communicated. By transferring ideas from the known realm to the unknown realm, truth is learned in the unknown realm by what is known in the known realm. Thus the principal function of figures of speech is to communicate ideas. Whether the figure be simple or complex, it has this same basic function.

There are several different figures in Scripture referred to as "parable." In the Old Testament, for example, the Hebrew word *mashal*, which is sometimes translated "parable," is actually used in many different senses. Good counsel or wise advice is referred to as parable (Num. 23:18; Job 27:1; Pss. 49:4; 78:2) when it is contrasted to the foolishness of a fool (Prov. 26:7, 9). A prophetic message was called a parable (Num. 24:15), as was a message of judgment (Mic. 2:4; Hab. 2:6). The nation to whom Ezekiel delivered his message dismissed his warnings and exhortations, saying, "Isn't he just telling parables?" (Ezek. 20:49). It is noted that even though the Old Testament uses the word parable in a wide range of meanings, central to each is the thought of communicating an idea from the speaker to the hearer.

In the New Testament also, the word "parable" is used of many different figures of speech. A parable may be in the form of a simile, which is a stated likeness. Jesus said, "I am sending you

11

out like sheep among wolves. Therefore be as shrewd as snakes and as innocent as doves" (Matt. 10:16). The use of "like" or "as" identifies a figure as a simile.

The parable may take the form of a metaphor, which is an implied likeness. For example, Jesus said, "I am the gate for the sheep" (John 10:7).

The parable may take the form of a similitude. In this figure transference is made from common knowledge. It is based on what is generally done rather than on what a certain individual actually did. When Christ said, "The kingdom of heaven is like yeast that a woman took and mixed into a large amount of flour until it worked all through the dough" (Matt. 13:33), He was using a similitude. Any individual familiar with the bread-baking process can learn truth through these words because the procedure is so commonly used.

The parable may take the form of a story. Instead of transferring truth on the basis of what people generally do as in the similitude, the story-parable is specific; it transfers truth involving a specific incident and calls attention to what one person did. Thus Jesus introduced three parables as follows: "There was a man who had two sons" (Luke 15:11), "There was a rich man" (Luke 16:1), and "In a certain town there was a judge" (Luke 18:2). The story-parable was the figure Christ used most commonly to teach truth to His hearers.

Because they also teach by transference, proverbs were sometimes referred to as parables (e.g., Luke 6:39). In Luke 4:23 the word *parabole* is translated "proverb." Other applications of the basic meaning of *parabole* are "lesson" (Matt. 24:32; Mark 13:28), "illustration" (Heb. 9:9), and "figuratively speaking" (11:19).

We also find the story-parable in the Old Testament. In order to pass judgment on David for his sin with Bathsheba, Nathan used a story-parable, reconstructing in it the record of David's sin (2 Sam. 12:1–4). This story-parable anticipated the form of many of our Lord's parables.

Although each of the above parables differs, they are all alike in that the truth to be learned is based on transference from reality. The content is always familiar and in the range of possibility.

In a parable no attempt is made to transfer from an unknown realm to another unknown realm; the transference is always from a known realm to the unknown.

In an allegory, in contrast to a parable, a story is constructed that is not based on reality. Communication through an allegory, then, does not depend on an objective reality but on the subjective use of imagination by the hearer. There are several examples of allegorical communication in the Old Testament. Ezekiel was commanded, "Set forth an allegory and tell the house of Israel a parable" (Ezek. 17:1). The prophet desired to trace Nebuchadnezzar's invasion of Jerusalem and the subsequent deportation of the people to Babylon. He did so by constructing an allegory in which an eagle broke off the top of a cedar tree and carried it away and replanted it in a new land. This whole narrative is an allegory, for it is contrary to nature. In it eagles do what eagles do not normally do. In order to make the nation understand the allegory, the prophet had to interpret its message.

Another illustration of an allegory is found in Judges 9. The citizens of Shechem had crowned Abimelech as their king. When Jotham heard of their action, he reproved them by constructing an allegory. He pictured the trees of the forest as seeking a king. They invited the olive tree to be king, but the olive refused. Then they invited the fig tree to be king, and the fig tree also refused. They then turned to the vine with the same invitation, but the vine refused too. Finally, they came to the thornbush and invited it to be king. The thornbush consented on condition that the trees would submit to its authority. By this allegory Jotham revealed that the people of Shechem had chosen the lowest among them to be their king. This story is an allegory because it is not based on reality. It is contrary to nature, for real trees do not act as the trees acted in the story. Truth is not conveyed, then, in an allegory by transference from the known realm to an unknown realm. The perception of truth through the allegory rests on the ingenuity of the hearer rather than on the logical transference of truth from the real world to the unknown realm. An allegory is constructed so as to teach truth through each individual part of the allegory. This requires the interpreter of an allegory to be concerned with every detail. In contrast, a parable is designed to teach one essential truth; the details of a parable may be merely incidental. Let us note that the Lord Jesus Christ did not use allegories as figures to transfer truth.

CHRIST'S USE OF PARABLES

Throughout His ministry, Christ put great stress on the importance of His words. Along with His miracles, His words constituted a major proof of His person (John 8:28; 14:10). Approximately one-third of Christ's teaching as recorded in the Gospels was in the form of parables. The question must be faced, then, as to why Christ used this method of conveying truth so extensively.

Christ Himself explained why He employed parables in His teaching (Matt. 13:10-17). He did so after speaking the parable of the sower, the seed, and the soils; at that time the disciples asked, "Why do you speak to the people in parables?" (v. 10). Their question implied that they recognized He was employing a new teaching method. Their question is interesting in the light of the fact that Christ, in the course of His ministry, had previously used a number of parables, although not of the extended story-parable type. Christ explained His use of the story-parables, saying, "The knowledge of the secrets of the kingdom of heaven has been given to you, but not to them. Whoever has will be given more, and he will have an abundance. Whoever does not have, even what he has will be taken from him. This is why I speak to them in parables: 'Though seeing, they do not see; though hearing, they do not hear or understand.' In them is fulfilled the prophecy of Isaiah: 'You will be ever hearing but never understanding; you will be ever seeing but never perceiving;'" (Matt. 13:11-14). Christ explained, on the one hand, that He used the parabolic method in His teaching to reveal truth to some but, on the other hand, He used it to hide truth from others. A mixed audience attended His teaching; some were believers and others were unbelievers. Some had placed faith in His person and His offer, but others had rejected His offer of Himself as Messiah. It was impossible to segregate the two groups. Christ wanted to instruct believers, but He did not want to add more responsibility to unbelievers by imparting truth to them for which they would be held responsible.

John the Baptist had appeared to the covenant nation as the prophet from God whose ministry was to introduce the Messiah to them. He called on the people to repent and thus to prepare themselves to meet the Messiah and be received into His kingdom. Their fruits of righteousness would show the genuineness of their repentance. When John had completed his introductory ministry, Christ publicly offered Himself as the Messiah to the waiting nation (Matt. 4:17). He authenticated His offer of Himself as the Messiah and His offer of the covenanted kingdom by the miracles that He performed. Matthew 8-11 records some of the validating miracles that Christ offered to the nation. During this period Christ told only a few parables.

A watershed in the earthly life of Christ was reached in Matthew 12. At this point, because Christ delivered a demon-possessed man who was blind and mute, the people expressed their willingness to accept Him as Savior and Sovereign, saying, "Could this be the Son of David?" (v. 23). In the Greek the question expects a negative answer; nevertheless, the evidence Christ presented was so sufficient that the people would have accepted Him as the Messiah if only the leaders had given approval. Faced with this attitude toward Christ, the Pharisees offered an alternative explanation. Denying that Christ received His power from God and was the Messiah sent from God, they said He received His power from Satan and therefore could not be Israel's Messiah. The unbelief of Israel's leaders on this occasion anticipated that nation's ultimate rejection of Christ that would culminate in His death on the cross. Christ presented three proofs to show that He did not get His power from Satan (vv. 25–29). He sounded a severe warning, affirming that if the nation persisted in believing the interpretation of the Pharisees, they would come under severe judgment (vv. 30–32). The Pharisees then challenged Christ to verify that He had come from heaven by presenting proof that they could not attribute to Satan. Christ's response was to offer the sign of Jonah. Christ's resurrection following His death would be a sign that Satan could not duplicate, and hence it would authenticate Him as Israel's Messiah. The record of the conflict with the Pharisees closes with the note that Christ's mother and brothers were on the fringes of the crowd and desired to speak to Him. Christ ignored their request because it was based on their physical relationship to Him. They were bound to Him by blood ties. Christ's present purpose was to show that a spiritual relationship of faith was necessary. Therefore he rejected those who would claim a relationship to Him by blood ties. "Pointing to his disciples, he said, 'Here are my mother and my brothers. For whoever does the will of my Father in heaven is my brother and sister and mother'" (vv. 49–50). An indication was thus given in Matthew 12 that the nation was in the process of rejecting Christ and would finally repudiate Him by crying for His death. Christ in turn indicated that He was setting the nation aside and withdrawing from that generation the offer of the kingdom that He had been making. The Davidic form of the theocracy would be postponed until some future time when He would return in power and glory to reign.

The conclusion that the Davidic form of the theocracy is in a state of postponement explains why Christ desired to communicate truth concerning the theocratic kingdom program to those who had put faith in His person and consequently belonged to Him. If Christ had spoken without the use of figures, both believers and unbelievers would have heard and understood what He said. Unbelievers would have incurred to themselves greater judgment because they would have sinned against additional light. Christ therefore chose the parabolic method of teaching. By using parables Christ could hide truth from unbelievers so as to free them from the responsibility that added knowledge would bring; at the same time He could convey truth to believers.

The vast majority of Christ's parables were spoken from this point in His life on to the end. While there may be miracles occurring between this notice of Christ's rejection and the Crucifixion, those miracles were not designed to convince the nation that Jesus was the Messiah. Their significance must be understood in the light of Israel's irreversible state of rejection. The miracles were designed to convey truth to believers, who might then be taught by both the words and the works of Christ.

THE INTERPRETATION OF PARABLES

When Christ told parables designed to convey truth to believers, He expected the believers to understand the parables, make the necessary transference from the parables, and to perceive the truth that He was seeking to convey. It is interesting to note that of all the parables delivered after the leaders registered their rejection of Christ as Messiah (Matt. 12), only two parables were interpreted by Christ. They were the parable of the sower, the seed, and the soils and the parable of the weeds. Since this was a new method of communicating truth, Christ interpreted these two parables to set a pattern of interpretation for all His parables. The fact that He did not interpret His subsequent parables indicates that He fully expected His hearers to understand what He taught. This is interesting in the light of the current confusion that exists as to the truth Christ intended to convey through His parables and the variety of interpretations given to them.

In order to properly interpret the parables, one must observe certain principles. The first principle, one that the Lord Himself stated, is that the parables concerned "the kingdom of heaven" (Matt. 13:11). The kingdom of heaven is that sphere over which the sovereign God rules. God as Sovereign has the right to delegate authority in the administration of His theocracy. In Old Testament times the theocracy was administered at different times in different ways. When Adam was in the Garden of Eden, God ruled directly over him. God assigned authority to Adam, whom He expected to exercise dominion in His name. After the Fall God ruled indirectly through the conscience, which witnessed that God's law was written on the hearts of people (Rom. 2:15). Following the Flood, God ruled through human government, charging governors with the responsibility of maintaining law and order and providing an atmosphere in which righteous people might live in peace. It was the responsibility of government administrators to exercise God's authority, even though this involved the death of a lawless one (Rom. 13:1–7). With the choice of Abraham, God's plan was for His theocracy to be developed within the nation that would spring from the patriarch's loins and be extended throughout the world through that nation. God assigned authority to patriarchs, judges, kings, and prophets as administrators in His kingdom. During this period God promised that the final theocratic Administrator would emerge from David's line and that He would occupy David's throne and rule over David's kingdom (2 Sam. 7:16). Thus the covenant people were anticipating the millennial kingdom as the ultimate form of the theocracy. However, it was not clearly revealed in the Old Testament that the nation would repudiate Messiah and condemn Him to death when He came and offered Himself to the covenant nation as the King in order to fulfill the covenant by establishing the kingdom. Because of the rejection of Messiah, the Davidic form of the theocracy had to be postponed. God's plan was that in the present age between Israel's rejection and future reception of Messiah, a new form of the theocracy would unfold. This new form was not to be the theocracy's ultimate form but, rather, an intermediate form. When Christ in Matthew 13:11 mentioned "the secrets of the kingdom of heaven," He was referring to new features about the theocracy that were unforeseen in the Old Testament but that would be revealed through His teaching. It is important to note that a great body of Christ's teaching through parables concerns itself with this new form of the theocracy, that is, the kingdom of heaven. Many of the Lord's parables begin with these words: "The kingdom of heaven is like" (cf. Matt. 13:24, 31 et al.), indicating further that the theocratic kingdom program is primarily in view in the parables. Because the church program is developed within the time bounds covered by the parables, and because the church is a part of the theocratic kingdom program, many interpreters have erroneously applied the parables directly to the church (as though they were primarily applicable to the church). However, we must remember that the parables were spoken to reveal truth concerning the broader theocratic kingdom program.

A second important principle in interpretation is to observe the immediate context. Parables were never spoken in a vacuum. In each instance that Christ spoke a parable, He was explaining some question or problem that His hearers were facing. Each parable thus was designed to solve a problem or to answer a question. For instance, the parable of the persistent friend (Luke 11:5–7) was Christ's response when a disciple asked, "Lord, teach us to pray" (v. 1). The parable of the rich man and Lazarus (Luke 16:19–31) was spoken because the Pharisees "loved money, . . . and were sneering at Jesus" (v. 14). This principle will apply to all parables whether the question or problem is stated, implied, or only recognized by Christ Himself. The interpreter, then, must search the immediate context to discover the problem or question to which Christ was addressing Himself. When this is discovered, the interpreter may then proceed with the interpretation, which in turn must provide an answer to the problem. If the answer does not suit the question or problem, the interpreter has either misunderstood the question or misinterpreted the parable.

This principle will set bounds on the interpretation. It will prevent an exercise in ingenuity or curb flights of fancy in interpretation. The part of the parable that contributes to the answer of the fundamental question or problem may be interpreted. And those aspects that would be extraneous and make no contribution to the solution may be ignored. There may be rare occasions when the problem or question is not evident until after the parable is interpreted; then, however, by searching the context the interpreter can usually find some indication of the problem or question that produced the parable.

When one has defined the broad context and has found a limit to the interpretation of the parable from the immediate context, one may proceed to interpret the parable itself. This will lead to a third important principle of interpretation; namely, the parable itself must be studied to determine what is the point at issue. For instance, in the parable of the persistent widow (Luke 18:1–8), the emphasis is not on the character of the judge but rather on the persistence of the widow. If undue attention is given to the character of the judge, then the parable will be misinterpreted. We must then sift out what is germane from the mass of details in the parable.

There is a fourth principle. Since a parable transfers truth from the known to the unknown realm, the interpreter must study the item or matter in the parable to which allusion is made and from which truth is to be transferred. One cannot interpret the parable of the sower unless one thoroughly understands the process of sowing seeds. One cannot understand the parable of new wine in old wineskins unless one is thoroughly familiar with the process of making wine in Christ's day. It is impossible to discover the truth in a parable by superimposing our culture on the culture of Christ's environment. The interpreter of parables, then, must become thoroughly conversant with the history, geography, culture, and customs of biblical times. One must learn to think as did those who lived in the Lord's day. Thus a biblical encyclopedia or a book on biblical customs will be an invaluable tool to help in the interpretation of parables. A difficulty we face in our day in interpreting parables is in understanding the frames of reference in which the parables are set. These must be clearly seen before we can understand the parables. Those who heard Christ had no such problems, for they lived in that culture and were thoroughly familiar with it. There was no need for the Lord to explain to them the things to which He referred and around which He built His parables. In order for us to be good interpreters, we must try to become as familiar with the culture, customs, and daily life of Palestine as were those who heard Christ.

When one has attained this familiarity, one may proceed to interpret the parables. From a knowledge of the structure and function of a door or gate, the interpreter will understand what

Christ meant when He said, "I am the gate" (John 10:7). The interpreter will know that Christ was revealing that He is the way of access to God and that He provides safety and security for those who come to God through Him. Further, the interpreter will know that those who enter into that security will find freedom and can go in and out. The one who has become thoroughly familiar with the work of the shepherd will understand that when Christ said, "I am the good shepherd" (v. 14), He was revealing that He claimed believers as His own; and He will guide them, guard, them, feed them, and provide for them according to their individual needs. From this it is obvious that before one can discern such a teaching through the figure, one must have a knowledge of the literal figure. The literal truth that can be learned from a parable depends on a literal interpretation of the antecedent in the parable itself. The use of a figure of speech does not necessitate a figurative or nonliteral interpretation. Rather, figurative language demands a literal interpretation from the known realm to the unknown if the truth of the figure is to be ascertained.

With these simple yet necessary principles in mind, we are ready to proceed to a study of the parables. In each instance the context will be studied; then in the light of the context we will seek to discover the question or problem, either expressed, implied, or discerned, that the parable answers; and, finally, we will interpret the parable so as to answer the question or problem. The interpretation may then be tested to see whether it answers the question that produced the parable.

THE PHYSICIAN
Luke 4:23

THE SETTING

After an extensive ministry in Jerusalem, Jesus returned to Nazareth; as was His custom on the Sabbath, He went to the local synagogue. On this occasion He was afforded the courtesy normally extended to a visiting rabbi—He was given the honor of reading from the Scriptures. The selected portion that He read was the messianic portrait found in Isaiah 61:1-2. Instead of returning to His seat, Christ assumed the role of a rabbi and sat down to interpret the Scripture that He had read. He declared that this messianic prophecy had that day been fulfilled, saying, "Today this scripture is fulfilled in your hearing" (Luke 4:21).

THE PROBLEM

Those in the synagogue were amazed. It was inconceivable to them that the Messiah would introduce Himself to Israel in such an insignificant place as Nazareth. They doubted Jesus' claim because they considered Him to be merely Joseph's son, and they thought the son of a carpenter could scarcely be the Messiah of Israel. Jesus' claim, then, raised a question concerning the person of Christ in the minds of those in the synagogue. Who is this who has made this claim? They wanted some proof that Jesus was the Messiah He claimed to be.

THE SOLUTION

Knowing the unexpressed turmoil and doubt in the minds of His hearers, Christ said, "Surely you will quote this proverb to me: 'Physician, heal yourself!'" (Luke 4:23). The Greek word translated "proverb" here is usually rendered "parable" in the New Testament (cf. Matt. 13:3, 19 et al.). It is the function of a physician to heal the sick. He does not minister to those who are well. The proverb recognized that if one claims to be able to heal the sick, that one should be able to heal personal infirmities. And

23

one who could not heal oneself would not be sought by those suffering from the same malady.

John the Baptist, the forerunner of the Messiah, addressed the nation, saying, "Repent, for the kingdom of heaven is near" (Matt. 3:2). In His public ministry Christ proclaimed the same message (4:17). John passed judgment on the nation, calling them a "brood of vipers" (Luke 3:7). Vipers were unclean animals, according to Moses' law. Thus John was viewing the nation as sinful and unclean under Israel's law and in the sight of God. John exhorted, "Produce fruit in keeping with repentance" (v. 8). John applied his message to people in all walks of life (vv. 10-14). John's message was widely disseminated, and without doubt those sitting in the synagogue at Nazareth on this occasion understood that they were in need of cleansing.

Jesus was considered by the people of Nazareth to be the illegitimate son of Joseph. That is why they asked, "Isn't this Joseph's son?" (Luke 4:22). When Jesus entered into conflict with the leaders of the nation, they said, "We are not illegitimate children" (John 8:41), and their inference was "as you are." Thus the people considered Jesus to be a sinner even as they were, and consequently they saw Him as in need of cleansing. That is why, during His conflict with the leaders, Christ asked, "Can any of you prove me guilty of sin?" (John 9:46). Thus in the synagogue on this occasion, the thinking of the people was that this self-proclaimed Messiah should do Messiah's work. If He was really the Messiah, He should grant cleansing and forgiveness of sin for the nation. He should demonstrate that He had fruits worthy of repentance, even as John had called for. If He could prove Himself to be clean, then they would feel warranted in accepting His message and turning to Him for forgiveness.

In desiring to see the miracles that Christ had performed earlier in Capernaum, the people were asking for confirmation through miracles that He was what He claimed to be. Christ, however, refused to perform miracles but invited them to put faith in His person. They needed the quality of faith demonstrated by the widow in Zarephath and Naaman the Syrian to whom God's prophets were sent (Luke 4:26-27). Without signs, the people would not believe Christ's claim; so they sought to kill Him by throwing Him down a cliff. Thus in this proverb-parable, Christ recognized the people's admission of their own need of cleansing, their knowledge that cleansing will come through the Messiah, and their skepticism of His claim to be the Messiah. As He departed from the crowd He anticipated the day when the nation would reject His person even as these people had rejected Him.

THE PATCHED GARMENT AND THE WINESKINS

Matthew 9:16–17; Mark 2:21–22; Luke 5:36–39

THE SETTING

The practice of fasting was prevalent in Israel. It was coupled with prayer as a sign of devotion to and dependence on God. It had degenerated among the Pharisees into an external observance used to impress people with the piety of the one fasting. The practice of fasting was adopted by John and his disciples and was practiced, not in the manner of the Pharisees, but as a sign of their faith in John's message that the Messiah who would grant forgiveness of sin was at hand. Their fasting, consequently, was a confession of their need of cleansing.

THE PROBLEM

The Pharisees constantly observed Christ and His disciples to see whether they conformed to Pharisaic traditions and practices. They observed that neither Christ nor His disciples fasted. The Pharisees recognized the relationship between John the Baptist and Jesus. Since John fasted, the Pharisees challenged Christ as to why neither He nor His disciples fasted.

THE SOLUTION

In order to answer this question, Christ used the figure of a marriage feast. Following the presentation of the bride to the bridegroom, the bridegroom appeared with his bride before the assembled guests who had been invited to celebrate the wedding at a marriage feast. This feast was a time of joy and rejoicing. Christ pictured Himself as the bridegroom, and He pictured that generation as guests who had been invited to a wedding. Those who had accepted the bridegroom's invitation to the wedding banquet would come in joy to rejoice with the bridegroom. Thus Christ was saying that in offering Israel the kingdom, He was

26

inviting people to share His joy. Consequently, at that time there should not be mourning.

This, in turn, raised two other significant questions. What was the relationship between what John and Jesus were offering the nation in announcing that the kingdom was at hand? Also, what had been presented to them under the guise of Pharisaism? The parable begins with an old, worn-out garment, one that was worthless and useless in its present condition. It would be possible to patch such a garment and prolong its usefulness for a short season. In order to do so, one would not cut a piece out of a new garment. Should one foolishly do so, one would destroy the new garment or render it useless. Further, new garments were made of undressed cloth that shrank with the first washing; therefore, should a new patch be sewn on an old garment, the new patch would shrink and tear away from the old garment in the process of washing. Then the hole would be larger than before. This would lead to the destruction of the old garment.

To further illustrate the truth, Christ used the figure of wineskins made from the skins of sheep or goats. There was a great deal of elasticity in a new wineskin. Since there was considerable expansion in the fermentation process, grape juice was put into new wineskins that would expand as the grape juice was transformed into wine. Sufficient elasticity would be retained for several years, and so the wineskin could be used again and again. When the wineskin became old, it lost its elasticity. If grape juice was put into an old, inflexible wineskin, the expansion of the fermentation process would destroy that wineskin. Thus not only would the wine be lost but the wineskin would be destroyed. Old wineskins were not cast away but were used as water bottles.

By these two parables Christ was showing that the old system propagated by Pharisaism was worthless, useless, and outdated. It was impossible to patch it up so that it could continue to be used. Christ had not come to reform Pharisaism but to introduce an entirely new doctrine into the life of the nation. Any attempt to superimpose the new doctrine on the old system would not only destroy the old system but the new as well. Thus Christ was putting a gulf between Himself and Pharisaism. Christ had previously done this when He said to His hearers, "I tell you that unless your righteousness surpasses that of the Pharisees and teachers of the law, you will certainly not enter the kingdom of heaven" (Matt. 5:20).

Christ anticipated the response of the Pharisees to His offer of the kingdom and the new doctrine that accompanied it when He said, "No one after drinking old wine wants the new, for he says, 'The old is better'" (Luke 5:39). The Pharisees were content with their system and had no desire to change. These parables set forth the irreconcilable differences between Christ and Pharisaism.

THE BLIND GUIDES
Matthew 7:3–5; Luke 6:39–42

The Pharisees, with their experts and teachers of the law, claimed to have the most authoritative voice in Israel in matters pertaining to Moses' law. Christ recognized this claim when He said, "The teachers of the law and the Pharisees sit in Moses' seat" (Matt. 23:2). The Pharisees demanded explicit submission to their teachings, but Christ warned against following them because of the disparity between their teachings and their lives (v. 3). In order to be able to teach, one must personally know and accept the truth that one propounds. Because of this fact our Lord spoke the parable "Can a blind man lead a blind man?" (Luke 6:39).

THE PROBLEM

In the Sermon on the Mount, Christ had rejected Pharisaism as the means by which one might attain righteousness that would fit him for entrance into the kingdom that He, as Messiah, had been offering. Christ had said, "I tell you that unless your righteousness surpasses that of the Pharisees and the teachers of the law, you will certainly not enter the kingdom of heaven" (Matt. 5:20). Two questions then arose: Why cannot Pharisaism bring one into the kingdom? What is the peril of following Pharisaism? The answer given in the proverb-parable was that the Pharisees were blind.

In the prologue to his gospel, John viewed the nation as being in darkness: "The light shines in the darkness, but the darkness has not understood it" (John 1:5). Christ came as light into the midst of darkness to dispel the darkness. Darkness symbolizes ignorance of God, while light symbolizes knowledge of God. Christ came to reveal God to people: "No one has ever seen God, but God the only Son, who is at the Father's side, has made him known" (v. 18). The revelation that Christ made of the Father

29

becomes light to believers. Those in darkness are blind. A teacher who is ignorant of God cannot lead others who are ignorant to a knowledge of God any more than a blind man can lead a blind man.

Christ showed the peril facing the nation if they kept following their blind leaders. He asked, "Will they not both fall into a pit?" (Luke 6:39). Both the leaders and the followers would perish. Since a student cannot progress beyond the knowledge of the teacher, the Israelites would remain in ignorance if they followed leaders who were ignorant of God.

THE SOLUTION

Christ gave a solution to the problem of blindness in the leaders. He instructed them to remove the cause of blindness from their own eyes, and then they would be able to instruct the blind who followed them. The Lord used the figure of a plank and a speck of sawdust from the plank. The speck of sawdust and the plank did not differ in nature, but only in size. The speck of sawdust irritated the eye but the plank produced blindness. Christ's accusation was that the professed teachers were concerned with small things in the lives of their followers but were unconcerned with the thing that had produced blindness in themselves. The teachers professed to be able to remove the irritant from the eyes of listeners while ignoring the blindness in themselves. The solution, then, was for the Pharisees to remove the cause of blindness in themselves; then they would be able to teach others who depended on them for guidance. In this case their blindness could be removed only by receiving light from the One who is the Light of the World, the Messiah, who stood in their midst.

THE WISE AND FOOLISH BUILDERS
Matthew 7:24–29; Luke 6:43–49

THE SETTING

Multitudes had been attracted to Christ because of His words and works. What Christ said and the miracles He performed aroused great interest in His message, "The kingdom of heaven is near" (Matt. 4:17). These multitudes knew from the Old Testament that righteousness was a prerequisite for entrance into the Messiah's kingdom (Ps. 24:3–4; Ezek. 36:25–29). They knew only the righteousness propounded by the Pharisees, but the Pharisaic standard had not satisfied them; they were not convinced that they were sufficiently righteous to enter the Messiah's kingdom. As they came together there was in their mind the question as to what kind of righteousness was necessary to enter the Messiah's kingdom.

In speaking the Beatitudes Christ had given the characteristics of a righteous person (Matt. 5:3–14). Christ then proceeded to use the law lawfully and interpret the law that they knew to show God's standard of righteousness (Matt. 5:17–48). While the Pharisees were concerned only with external conformity to the law, Christ demanded internal as well as external righteousness. In His interpretation of the Old Testament law, our Lord went far beyond the commonly accepted interpretation of the religious leaders of the day. His principle was that righteousness is revealed in what a person thinks as well as in what a person does. Christ next gave guidance as to the kind of life that those who are eligible to enter the kingdom should display (Matt. 6:1–7:12). Having set aside Pharisaism as a basis for entering the kingdom (Matt. 5:20) and having held up the holiness of God that was revealed in the law as the standard of righteousness for entrance, Christ closed His discourse with an invitation to enter the kingdom. Christ did not appeal to His hearers to depend on the teaching of the Pharisees, but rather to have faith in His words. The truth that He enunciated was pictured as a "narrow gate"

31

(Matt. 7:13). Christ contrasted this narrow gate and the teaching of the Pharisees, which He viewed as a wide gate and a broad road. Thus He taught that faith in His word, would lead to life, but obedience to the Pharisees' words would lead to destruction.

THE PROBLEM

Out of this instruction arose a question: Why is it important to make a decision concerning the words of Christ, and what is the danger in rejecting them? Early in His public ministry, Christ had called on the nation to make a decision concerning both His person and the truth that He taught (cf. Luke 4:16–21). Thus the people were held responsible for the revelation of the Father that Christ gave to them.

THE SOLUTION

In order to answer this question, Christ pictured His hearers as builders. Everyone who heard His words was responsible for those words. The truth that Christ presented was a foundation not only for life in this age but for the coming age. The permanence of any building depends on its foundation. The building that every person builds will be subjected to a test. Christ used the picture of floods that came as a result of rains and storms. If a building rested on a solid foundation, it would stand against any flood tide that came. On the other hand, if one had neglected to lay a sound foundation and had built on sand, that person's building would collapse when the floods came and the storms blew; and the reason would be that it had no foundation.

In this way Christ contrasted His words with Pharisaic teaching. The Pharisees did not have the truth of God; therefore, those who followed them were building without an adequate foundation. At the time of judgment to determine who would enter the Messiah's kingdom, all that had been built on the sand would be swept away. Such builders would lose their part in the kingdom. Conversely, those who heard and believed the words concerning the Father that Christ taught would at the time of judgment already have provided a secure foundation. Therefore, in the coming judgment they will be preserved and will experience the joys of the Messiah's kingdom. Thus our Lord taught that the eternal destiny of people depends on a proper response to the revelation of the Father that He was giving and to the offer of Himself as Messiah to the nation of Israel.

CHILDREN IN THE MARKETPLACE
Matthew 11:16–19; Luke 7:29–35

THE SETTING

The ministry of John the Baptist was controversial and his baptism divided the nation of Israel. "All the people, even the tax collectors, when they heard Jesus' words, acknowledged that God's way was right, because they had been baptized by John. But the Pharisees and the experts in the law rejected God's purpose for themselves, because they had not been baptized by John" (Luke 7:29–30). Thus we know Christ was facing continued opposition to Himself and the offer of the Davidic kingdom to that nation.

THE PROBLEM

The Pharisees and their experts in the law were recognized as teachers in Israel, but they were not turning to John in repentance to identify themselves with the coming Messiah. On the other hand the common people, including the tax collectors, who were considered along with harlots as the lowest strata of society, were flocking to John and receiving his baptism in anticipation of the establishment of the messianic kingdom. This difference in response raised the question of why the leaders did not accept John's message and turn in faith to the One whom John was introducing.

THE SOLUTION

In order to answer the question, Christ likened the Pharisees and the experts in the law to children playing in the marketplace. He called attention here, not to the games that the children were playing, but rather to a chief characteristic of children—insistence on having their own way. The children in the parable insisted that when they asked their playmates to dance, they expected them to dance; when the children paraded in a funeral procession, they expected their playmates to fall in line. Christ

was saying that the Pharisees were like children in that they
wanted to be followed no matter where they might lead their
followers. Further, Christ's parable reminds that it is natural for
children to rebel against authority. If someone asks children to
dance, they will mourn; if someone asks children to mourn, they
will rejoice.

When John called for repentance, the Pharisees exercised the
independence so characteristic of children and refused to do what
he said. They criticized Jesus when He set an example of rejoicing and asked those who had repented to join with Him in the joy
of the kingdom. When John called Israel to repentance, the
Pharisees likewise refused to repent. Christ "played the flute" and
John "sang a dirge" (Luke 7:32), but the Pharisees responded to
neither. Christ closed this teaching, saying enigmatically, "But
wisdom is proved right by all her children" (v. 35). Christ was
saying that whether He was right or the Pharisees were right
would be demonstrated in the lives of the two groups of followers.
Those who followed Him would evidence the fruits of righteousness, but such fruit would be lacking in the lives of those who
followed the teaching of the Pharisees.

THE TWO DEBTORS
Luke 7:41-50

Christ had been invited by a Pharisee to have dinner at his home, but the host's attitude was condescending. As the guests ate the meal a woman whose sinful life was well known entered the dining area. This would not have been unusual in a culture in which hospitality was considered a virtue, especially if the guest were considered inferior to the host. For such an occasion as this a Pharisee would set the table in an open place, perhaps in the courtyard. The host would leave open the front gate so that passers-by might not only observe the hospitality of the host, but even enter the courtyard to view the food that the host had provided for the guests. The more sumptuous the provision of the Pharisee, the more honor that would be heaped on that one as a host.

Thus the custom of that day made it possible for this sinful woman to come into the place where Christ was reclining at the meal. However, this woman did not come to observe but to pay homage to the Lord. She brought with her an alabaster jar of perfume. This very costly ointment possibly was purchased with her ill-gotten gains. The woman showed the attitude of her heart toward Christ by standing at His feet, which He would have extended away from the table in His reclining position. The woman began to bathe His feet with her tears. This was her way of telling Christ that she had repented. She was acknowledging her sinfulness and confessing her need of forgiveness from sin. Since the Messiah was the One who was to put away sin (Isa. 53:6; Zech. 13:1), the woman's tears not only were a sign of her sinfulness but of her faith in Christ as the Messiah. She had come seeking His forgiveness. After wetting His feet with the abundance of her tears, she used her hair as a towel and dried His feet. Then she showed her affection for Christ by kissing His feet. This suggests that she was confident that she already had received His forgiveness. She showed her adoration for His person by pouring perfume from the alabaster jar on His feet.

THE PROBLEM

According to Pharisaic tradition, ceremonial defilement was incurred if one was touched by a woman. Certainly, to have been touched by a woman of such a notorious reputation would have resulted in serious defilement. The Pharisees concluded that if Christ was what He claimed to be, the Messiah, He would have known the reputation of this woman because Messiah was to be a prophet (Deut. 18:15–18). He would have known all things, especially something as obvious as this woman's reputation, which was so well known to the others present. If Christ was the Messiah as He claimed to be, He would refrain from incurring such defilement. Thus a conflict arose in the minds of the Pharisees. On the one hand, the Pharisees knew that Jesus claimed to be the Messiah; on the other hand, they observed that He welcomed the sinful woman's touch that their tradition said would cause defilement. Who, then, was this person? And if He was what He claimed to be, why did He accept the woman's gift and her adoration?

THE SOLUTION

In order to answer this problem, Christ told the story of a money-lender to whom two men were in debt. One man owed nearly two years of wages, and the other owed two months of wages. Because neither was able to repay his indebtedness, the moneylender canceled the debts. While this was contrary to the nature of money-lenders, it was in perfect keeping with the character of God. Now Christ addressed a question to Simon the Pharisee: "Which of them will love him more?" (Luke 7:42). The Pharisee responded in the only logical way possible, saying that the one who had been forgiven the greatest debt would show the greatest devotion. Christ readily approved that conclusion.

Christ now contrasted the attitude of the Pharisee and that of the woman. The Pharisee had not invited Christ into his home to honor Him but rather to observe Him. Perhaps Simon even hoped to find some accusation he could lodge against Christ. The Lord was a guest in the Pharisee's house, but He had not been shown the courtesies that customary hospitality demanded. Normally a guest would have prepared for such a banquet by bathing at the public bath, anointing the body with oil, and putting on clean clothing. In traveling from the bath to the banquet hall, the guest's feet would have become soiled; so it would have been necessary to sponge the feet before reclining at the banquet table. Courtesy demanded that a basin of water be provided by the host. But Simon the Pharisee had made no such provision for Christ. Custom would have demanded that the host greet the guest with a kiss, even though hypocritical, as a profession of respect and affection. But the Pharisee had ignored these customary courtesies. The host was expected to provide a vial of oil so that the face of the guest might be anointed as a sign of joy because of the invitation to participate in the banquet. But no anointing oil had been provided for Christ. A woman had provided what the Pharisee had neglected to provide. Instead of washing Christ's feet with water from a basin, she washed them with tears. Instead of drying His feet with a towel, she wiped them with her hair. Instead of kissing Christ's cheek, she stooped to kiss His feet. And in place of the olive oil that normally was used to anoint the countenance, she lavished expensive perfume on Christ.

Simon's failure to show Christ the usual courtesies due a guest resulted from his lack of faith in the person of Christ. The woman's conduct was just the opposite of Simon's because of her faith in His person. Christ could therefore say to the woman, "Your sins are forgiven" (Luke 7:48). Lest anyone conclude that the woman's sins were forgiven because of her works, Christ explained, "Your faith has saved you; go in peace" (v. 50). Thus her works were not the basis of her salvation, but she was saved because of faith in the person of Christ that produced the works. By this parable Christ answered the question in the mind of the

Pharisee as to why He received the affection and adoration of the sinful woman. The parable teaches that He accepted what she offered because it sprang from her faith. The one who can demonstrate the genuineness of faith by the fruits of repentance is the one who receives forgiveness. Such a one is received and welcomed by Christ.

PARABLES PROVING THE PERSON OF CHRIST
Matthew 12:22–30; Mark 3:22–27

THE SETTING

Throughout the course of Christ's ministry there had been an increasing opposition to Him on the part of the religious leaders. Despite the fact that His words and works clearly demonstrated that He was the Messiah as He claimed, the religious leaders adamantly refused to believe or accept Him. The pressing question facing the nation throughout the life of Christ on earth was the matter of His person. Who was He? Was He the Messiah as He claimed to be? The population of Galilee seemed convinced that He was the Messiah, who would redeem Israel and reign over them. On this occasion Christ cast a demon from a man who was both blind and mute. The people responded, "Could this be the Son of David?" (Matt. 12:23). According to the Greek New Testament, their question expected a negative answer. However, the people did not give a negative answer because of a lack of solid evidence to confirm that Christ was who He claimed to be; rather, they phrased their question in this way because of the persistent opposition of the religious leaders. Mark noted that at this time some of the religious scholars had come from Jerusalem with the avowed purpose of dissuading the people from putting faith in Christ (Mark 3:22). Such an unusual display of power as had been witnessed on this occasion demanded an explanation. Certainly, such a work was not natural but obviously supernatural. There were just two sources of supernatural powers by which such a miracle might be performed. Either God or Satan had provided the power. The representatives of the Pharisees attributed the miracle to Satan, saying, "It is only by Beelzebub, the prince of demons, that this fellow drives out demons" (Matt. 12:24).

THE PROBLEM

Christ claimed that He performed His miracles by the power of God (John 14:10). The Pharisees claimed that He performed His miracles by the power of Satan. Thus the question arose as to which explanation was true. Had Jesus Christ come from God or from Satan? Since this miracle was performed in the demonic realm, Christ was claiming to have a greater power than Satan possesses. Christ answered this question by speaking in parables (Mark 3:23).

THE SOLUTION

In order to prove logically that He had greater power than Satan, as He had already demonstrated through the miracle, Christ gave three reasons showing why He was not energized by Satan. In the first of a series of three parables, Christ said that a kingdom divided against itself would be destroyed (Matt. 12:25–26). This principle is true not only for a kingdom but for a city and even for an individual household as well. Christ's argument was that if He received power from Satan and then used that power against Satan, the Devil would be destroying his own kingdom by giving Him power. Such was inconceivable, for no one would give another power for self-destruction.

In the second parable (Matt. 12:27–28), Christ used another argument. There were exorcists in Israel in that day (cf. 7:22). Those who cast out demons were not classified as "evildoers." Such exorcists were welcomed by the nation and were counted as God's gift to a people plagued with demon possession. The nation expressed its gratitude for such exorcists. Since the nation did not attribute this exorcism to Satan, Christ asked, "By whom do your people drive them out?" (Matt. 12:27). Christ's argument was based on the fact that they themselves recognized that not all exorcism was by Satan's power. What, then, made them conclude that He operated by Satan's power? Why could not He rightly operate by the power of God?

The third parable (Matt. 12:29) drew on the imagery of a secure household. Because of the value of the treasure within the household, the gates had been barred and guards posted to prevent a robbery. If a robber was determined in spite of the security to rob the household, the robber must be able to overpower the guard. If the guard was stronger than the robber, the goods would be secure. But if the robber was stronger than the guard, then the goods would be plundered. Christ's argument was that Satan would guard those who are his own. If Christ is able to deliver one from Satan's domain, this is evidence that He is stronger than Satan.

Thus in these three parables Christ answered the question of who He is. He also identified the One from whom He receives power and authority. The logic in the parables proved that He could not have originated from Satan and was not operating by Satan's power as the religious leaders claimed. He must have come from God. The logical conclusion of the parable was, in Christ's words, "If I drive out demons by the Spirit of God, then the kingdom of God has come upon you" (Matt. 12:28). Thus Christ's offer of the messianic kingdom to Israel and of Himself as the Messiah was valid.

THE EMPTY HOUSE
Matthew 12:43–45

THE SETTING

In the prior context some of the Pharisees and teachers of the law had said to Christ, "Teacher, we want to see a miraculous sign from you" (Matt. 12:38). This type of request suggests that some of the religious leaders who had heard Christ's refutation of the accusation that He operated by Satan's power were now questioning whether they were right in rejecting Him as Messiah. Thus they had come to ask Him for a sign that would demonstrate conclusively to their satisfaction that He was what He claimed to be. Christ refused to give them any additional signs other than the sign of Jonah, which was the coming evidence through His bodily Resurrection that He was the Messiah. Christ had already proved His authority in the realm of nature by stilling storms and walking on water. He had shown His power over sickness and disease by His many miracles of healing, and He had shown His power over Satan by casting out demons. He had demonstrated His power over death by restoring the dead to life, and He had shown His authority to forgive sin. If such evidence was rejected, no further evidence could be given that would satisfy the skeptics. Christ anticipated a forthcoming judgment on that generation (Matt. 12:41–43).

THE PROBLEM

The following questions naturally arose: What was the state of the nation now that it had rejected all the evidence offered by Christ concerning His person? How did God view that generation to whom the offer of the kingdom had been made through the ministry of John the Baptist and through Christ Himself?

THE SOLUTION

Christ spoke of a demon-possessed man. Such a one was considered unclean and unfit to live in the community. He would

43

have been compelled to separate himself from his family and village and live apart. In order to find a more suitable place in which to dwell, the demon left this man. Being freed from possession, the man now could return to his family, friends, and community and enjoy fellowship with them again.

However, the demon did not find a more suitable place and returned to the man from whom it had departed. The demon evidently suspected that its host would have been occupied by other demons in its absence; however, on returning it found the man still free from demon possession. The demon's former place of occupancy was "unoccupied, swept clean and put in order" (Matt. 12:44). What follows in the parable suggests that the demon left the man because of loneliness and to seek companionship with other demons. When the demon returned to the man, it brought seven other demons more wicked than itself and all entered into the man. Consequently, the man was again forced to withdraw from his family, friends, and community and to live in isolation. Thus as tragic as was the man's condition at the beginning, his final condition was worse. Instead of being host to one demon, he was now host to it and seven other demons, all of whom would seek to operate through him.

Christ's application was "That is how it will be with this wicked generation" (Matt. 12:45). John the Baptist in his ministry had addressed the sinful nation of Israel and called the people to repentance. As a result "the whole Judean countryside and all the people of Jerusalem went out to him. Confessing their sins, they were baptized by him in the Jordan River" (Mark 1:5). This profession of cleansing by the nation was represented in the parable by the departure of the demon from the demon-possessed man (Matt. 12:43). Although the disciples of John the Baptist had by their baptism professed to have faith in the coming of Messiah, they subsequently came under the influence of the unbelief of the leaders of Israel and turned from the Messiah. Thus the original profession of cleansing was only temporary, not permanent. If the nation of Israel had turned in faith to Christ, the cleansing initiated by John would have been made permanent and the people would have been delivered from their uncleanness. But now because of rejecting Christ, the nation that had professed through baptism their desire to experience cleansing was now in a worse state than before their profession. They were permanently separated from God because of their uncleanness. Permanent cleansing had been available but it was rejected.

PARABLES CONCERNING THE NEW FORM OF THE KINGDOM

THE SETTING

The accusation that Christ received His power from Satan (Matt. 12:24) was of watershed importance in the life of Christ. The rejection by the leaders anticipated the nation's final rejection that would culminate in Christ's death on the cross. Henceforth there was no question as to the rejection by Israel of Christ's offer of Himself as Messiah and of the offer of the messianic kingdom to Israel. Christ sounded a severe warning, saying, "Every sin and blasphemy will be forgiven men, but the blasphemy against the Spirit will not be forgiven. Anyone who speaks a word against the Son of Man will be forgiven, but anyone who speaks against the Holy Spirit will not be forgiven, either in this age or in the age to come" (Matt. 12:31–32). The miracles that Christ had performed proved that He was from God and that His works were done by the power of the Holy Spirit. Salvation was through Christ alone. People might come to faith in Him by His own words. If one rejected Christ's words, that one might come to faith in Christ by the testimony of the Father. If one rejected both the words of Christ and the testimony of the Father, that one might still come to faith in Christ to know salvation through the works of the Spirit performed through Him. If one rejected all three testimonies to the person of Christ, there was no added testimony that could be given in order to bring that one to faith in Christ and to salvation. The sin against the Spirit referred to here was possible only when Christ was personally present on earth and was offering Himself to Israel as Savior-Sovereign. This particular sin could only be committed when Christ was performing miracles to authenticate Himself before the nation.

Following this warning Christ served notice that this generation was under judgment because of their rejection of Him (Matt. 12:39–42).

46

This was followed by an incident that marked Christ's rejection of the nation. While Christ was speaking to a large crowd, He was informed that His mother and brothers were waiting to speak to Him (v. 47). Christ rejected their request. "Pointing to his disciples, he said, 'Here are my mother and my brothers. For whoever does the will of my Father in heaven is my brother and sister and mother'" (v. 49). A blood tie united Christ and His mother and brothers. In contrast, a tie of faith united Christ with His disciples. Christ rejected the claim of those who were united to Him only by blood and recognized the unity existing between Himself and those who put faith in Him. Thus Christ indicated that He was setting aside the nation of Israel, which is related to Him by descent from Abraham and was accepting those who were related to Him by faith. This incident is significant for it reveals that Israel as a nation was being set aside and a new relationship was being instituted with a people on the basis of faith rather than on the basis of physical descent.

THE PROBLEM

The nation of Israel had been bound to God by promise (Gen. 12:1–6; 13:14–17) and by covenant (15:18). God had chosen physical descendants of Abraham to be the people to whom He would reveal Himself and through whom He would make Himself known to the world (Exod. 19:6). Israel had started out as a theocracy and was the nation over which God ruled and through which His purposes would be accomplished as God. According to the promise that God gave to David, Israel was ultimately to be ruled over by a King who would be of Davidic descent (2 Sam. 7:16). The divine promise was that a descendant of David would sit on David's throne and rule over David's house. Consequently, the nation was anticipating a King who would rule over them. A major theme of the Old Testament prophetic books was truth about the Messiah and His kingdom and the peace and prosperity that awaited the nation. John the Baptist, the last of the Old Testament prophets, came to Israel with the glorious announcement that "the kingdom of heaven is near" (Matt. 3:2). Christ began His public ministry with the same proclamation (4:17). Christ had declared the standard of righteousness necessary for entrance into the kingdom and had shown how those who are subjects of the kingdom will live (Matt. 5–7). Christ then authenticated His offer of the kingdom to the nation by the multitude of miracles that He performed (Matt. 8–11). But the nation that had been living in the expectation of Messiah's reign rejected Christ, counting Him a demon-possessed lunatic. Without righteousness there could be no kingdom, and without obedience to God there could be no blessing (Deut. 28). It was thus necessary that the generation of Christ's day be set aside and the kingdom program be postponed that was to be developed in Israel. Christ spoke of this postponement many times in His parables.

From the beginning of creation there had always existed some form of God's kingdom on earth and some channel through which God demonstrated His right to rule. In the Garden of Eden a perfect miniature theocracy existed as long as Adam and Eve were in subjection to God. God ruled and delegated authority to Adam to rule as His representative (Gen. 1:26–27), and Adam exercised the rule delegated to him by God. After the Fall God ruled through conscience and sought to bring people into subjection to Himself (Rom. 2:15). When people rebelled against the authority of God exercised through conscience, God brought the judgment of the Flood and then instituted His rule through human government (Gen. 9:6; Rom. 13:1–7; 1 Peter 2:13–17). With the call of Abraham, God began to develop His rule in and through the nation of Israel. After the patriarchs (Exod. 4:16–7:1), God exercised His theocratic rule through the judges (Judg. 2:16–18; Acts 13:20) and finally through the kings, who ruled by divine appointment. The nation had to be set aside because of their disobedience. The northern kingdom fell to Assyria in 722 B.C., and Jerusalem was finally destroyed by Babylon in 586 B.C.

This discipline, however, did not abrogate the promises and covenants or remove from Israel the expectation that God's theocratic rule would be established under Messiah here on the earth. The record of the New Testament is that Christ came as that afore-promised Messiah and offered the covenanted kingdom to Israel. The nation willfully rejected Christ and repudiated His offer. Although the promise of God still stood, the institution of the kingdom was postponed. Now the following question arises: In what form would God administer His theocracy on earth in the interval between Israel's rejection of the messianic kingdom and Israel's future reception of the Messiah and His kingdom? The series of parables that Christ used were designed to describe the important features of the new and unexpected form in which the theocracy would be manifested in this present age. In Matthew 13:11 these parables are referred to as mysteries or "secrets of the kingdom." The Old Testament did not reveal that there would be an interval between the offer of the kingdom and Israel's enjoyment of the kingdom as a result of the rejection of Christ by the nation. The form in which the theocracy would be developed in the present age was unknown in the Old Testament, but now Christ saw fit to reveal through parables this new form of theocracy with its major characteristics.

It is to be stressed that when Christ revealed truth about the kingdom, He was not speaking about the church. When He spoke of the coming kingdom age, He was not speaking of the church age. The church began on the Day of Pentecost in Acts 2 and will continue on earth until the Rapture, an event that will precede the seven years of the Tribulation. The coming kingdom age of which Christ spoke began at the time of Israel's rejection of Him as Messiah and will continue until Israel's future reception of Him as Messiah at the Second Advent. The church is a part of the kingdom, but the kingdom is more extensive than just the church. The church age is within the new age of the kingdom, but the kingdom age extends beyond the church age. Thus the present parables do not primarily reveal truth about the church but rather about the kingdom of which the church is a part.

THE SOWER, THE SEED, AND THE SOILS
Matthew 13:3-23; Mark 4:3-25; Luke 8:15-18

THE SETTING

Since wheat was a staple of the diet in Palestine, the procedure of raising wheat would have been very familiar to the Lord's hearers. In preparation for sowing the seed, the ground was cleared of all old growth. This caused the entire field to look the same. The sower had no idea of what roots or rocks lay beneath the surface soil. The soil was not plowed as is done today, but rather the seed was broadcast by the sower on the surface of the soil. The seed was then scratched into the soil with a primitive wooden plow. The sowing was done before the early rains that caused the seed to germinate. The sower waited through the growing period for the coming of the latter rains that brought the grain to full fruition and thus provided a bountiful harvest.

THE PROBLEM

Christ, at the outset of this series of parables, faces the question of how the truth He is revealing will be disseminated and what response may be expected.

THE SOLUTION

The Lord Himself interpreted the parable to His hearers. He Himself was the sower, and the field represented those who heard His words (Matt. 13:37). Since the seed is referred to both as the "word of God" (Luke 8:12) and as "the sons of the kingdom" (Matt. 13:38), we see that the Word of God will be sown throughout the age through those who are counted as sons of the kingdom. Further, we see that the sower is good and the seed good and that the field gives prospect of a fruitful harvest. However, we note that there are varying responses to the same sowing by the same sower. The response does not depend on the sower or

50

on the seed but on the soil, that is, on the hearer. Some of the good seed was heard by those whom Christ likened to the footpath that bordered the field. This path would not have been plowed after the seed was scattered. The seed could easily be eaten by the birds. Christ likened other hearers to rocky soil. The underlying rock had only a thin layer of soil on it. The rock would absorb the sun's heat and cause the seed to germinate unusually fast and to have a rapid growth. However, there was not sufficient soil for the roots to grow. Any moisture the soil received would quickly evaporate, and there would be no moisture to sustain the original rapid growth. Therefore the new growth would quickly die. Christ likened other hearers to soil that is choked with thorns. Because the field had been purged of the previous year's growth, the sower would not know that underneath the soil were the roots of thorns. Consequently, when the good seed was sown, it grew up among thorns. The thorns soon choked out the wheat that was in its midst. Some of the good seed fell on good soil and was able to produce a bountiful harvest.

In interpreting the parable Christ explained what prevented the good seed sown by the sower from coming to fruition. The birds that ate the soil along the path represented Satan, who is antagonistic to the Word of God and seeks to prevent the seed from germinating or coming to harvest. The seed sown on the rocky place germinated but could not put down roots. Our Lord was explaining that lack of growth or lack of depth in the truth will cause a person to fall when persecution or testing comes. The seed that fell among thorns pictured the unfruitful life of one who is concerned with the pursuit of wealth, the cares of this life, or with material things. The good soil represented one who not only hears the Word but understands it. This process, as Jesus taught elsewhere (cf. John 16:13–14), is through the ministry of the Holy Spirit, who causes a person to understand and to appropriate and consequently live by the Word that has been received. Thus from this first parable in a series, we learn that in the present age there will be a sowing of the Word of God by our Lord (Luke 8:12) and by those whom He calls "the sons of the kingdom" (Matt. 13:38). There will be responses that vary, depending on the preparedness of the hearer. In spite of the lack of fruit among three classes of hearers, we are assured that there will be a bountiful harvest.

THE GROWING SEED
Mark 4:26–29

THE PROBLEM

Since in the previous parable Christ had stressed that sowing would be carried on throughout the age by "the sons of the kingdom" (Matt. 13:38), the question arose as to whether the harvest would depend on the skill and determination, the diligence, or the wisdom of the sowers. What would produce the harvest?

THE SOLUTION

In this parable like the previous parable, seed was scattered on the ground. There is no reason for the seed and the ground to have a meaning different from the previous parable. The parable emphasizes that the work of spreading the Word of God is entrusted to human agents. The additional truth now stressed was that after the sowing, the sower has nothing more to do until the harvest. "The seed sprouts and grows. . . . All by itself the soil produces grain" (Mark 4:27–28). Christ was emphasizing that life within the seed causes it to germinate, grow, and then to produce heads of grain. The harvest does not depend on the human agents who did the sowing but rather on the life within the seed. Growth occurs whether the sower is awake or asleep. The seed of itself produces grain. When the life of the seed has reproduced itself in the new grain, the sower then may participate in the harvest. The sower may gather the new grain but the sower cannot produce the harvest. This parable was given to reveal to those who will be sent to sow the Word that they must do their sowing in utter dependence on the power of the Word to produce its own fruit. The essential contribution of this parable to the unfolding of the kingdom program in the present age is to stress that while human agencies may disseminate the Word of God, fruitfulness will be the result of the Word itself, not the human agent.

53

THE WEEDS
Matthew 13:24-30

THE PROBLEM

Since Christ through "the sons of the kingdom" (Matt. 13:38) is active in the world sowing the Word of God, what will be Satan's activity during the course of this age? Are those who sow the seed to anticipate freedom from opposition by the evil one? Such questions find their answer in this parable.

THE SOLUTION

Once again Christ built on the familiar figure of a sower sowing good seed in a field. Since this parable was built on the previous parables, the interpretation of the sower, the seed, and the field are the same here as Christ had previously explained. What is added to the revelation of the course of the age in this parable is that after the good seed was sown, an enemy came and sowed the seed of weeds among the wheat. The enemy is explained as Satan himself, who vigorously opposes the Word and the work of God (Matt. 13:39). The weeds that Satan sows are called "the sons of the evil one" (v. 38). Just as through the course of the age Christ will work through those who are "the sons of the kingdom" (v. 38), so Satan will work through those who belong to him and become his instruments to oppose the Word of God. It is to be noted that during the period of germination and initial growth, it is impossible to distinguish between the wheat and the weeds. Not until harvest can it be determined which is which. The reason for this is that, in the initial stage of growth, the weeds resemble wheat. It is not until heads of grain begin to appear in the wheat plants that one can determine if weeds have been sown, for weeds do not produce grain. Since darnel has the characteristics of the weeds in the parable, Bible scholars generally feel it is the type of weed of which Christ was speaking.

In this parable, then, Christ revealed that there will be a false

54

counter-sowing by Satan alongside the good sowing of the Word. This sowing by Satan and its results will continue throughout the age. As the growing season progresses it will be apparent that weeds have been sown among the wheat. In the parable the servants suggested that they go through the field and pull up the weeds. It seemed to them a wise plan to try to separate the wheat from the weeds as soon as it became evident that there were weeds in the field. However, the owner of the servants instructed them to let the wheat and weeds grow side by side. The separation was not to be made until the harvest itself, for in seeking to remove the weeds, the servants also would have uprooted the wheat and consequently destroyed it. Christ saw the harvest as analogous to the end of the age. He explained, "The Son of Man will send out his angels, and they will weed out of his kingdom everything that causes sin and all who do evil. They will throw them into the fiery furnace, where there will be weeping and gnashing of teeth. Then the righteous will shine like the sun in the kingdom of their Father" (Matt. 13:41–43).

This parable, then, reveals that Satan will be active through his own throughout this present age. He will seek to prevent the Word of God that is being sown from coming to fruition and will remain active until the end of the age. At that time there will be a judgment to separate the sons of the kingdom from the sons of the evil one.

This separating judgment will be explained in later parables by the Lord.

THE MUSTARD SEED
Matthew 13:31–32

THE PROBLEM

Because of Satan's opposition to the sowing of the Word and his activity of disseminating evil, the question had to be faced as to what would come of the kingdom. Christ answered this important question in the parable of the mustard seed.

THE SOLUTION

The Lord likened the kingdom of heaven to a mustard seed, describing it as "the smallest of all your seeds" (Matt. 13:32). This reference has created problems in the minds of many who know from familiarity with the proverbial mustard seed that there are other seeds much smaller. This has raised questions as to the reliability of Christ's words. Light was shed on Christ's reference on one occasion when this author was visiting Israel. The guide took us to what appeared to be a tree some ten to twelve feet high and removed a seed pod. When he opened it, we saw the familiar mustard seed. Then the guide put that seed in the palm of his hand and crushed it with his thumb. What appeared to be a smudge of black dust spread out of the crushed seed. This dust was identified by the guide as the seed of the mustard. What we familiarly refer to as mustard seed is really a container for a multitude of seed. But perhaps a better explanation is that Christ was using a popular Jewish idiom. The diameter of a mustard seed was viewed as the smallest measurable and the weight of a mustard seed was seen as the smallest amount that could be weighed by using a balance. Thus Christ was emphasizing a small and insignificant beginning. The parable goes on to say that a mustard seed grows into a tree. We are not to think of the weed that spreads across our meadows and attains a height of twelve to eighteen inches. The Oriental mustard plant in one season can reach the height of a tree. This author has on hand a picture taken in Dallas of a mustard seed that in one year grew into a tree thirty-two feet in height. It truly was of sufficient size so that birds could nest within its branches. This part of the parable emphasizes a great discernible growth from an insignificant beginning. The symbolism of the birds lodging in the branches can be understood by referring to similar imagery used in Daniel 4. In his vision Nebuchadnezzar saw a great tree of enormous height, and birds came and dwelled in the branches (Dan. 4:10–12). The fruit of the tree fed the birds that lodged in it, as well as feeding the beasts that took refuge under it. In interpreting the vision to Nebuchadnezzar, Daniel explained that the tree represented Nebuchadnezzar's kingdom and the birds and the beasts represented those nations that received benefit from Nebuchadnezzar's rule. In applying the interpretation of Daniel's tree vision to the present parable, we can see that Christ was teaching that though the new form of the kingdom would begin with an insignificant beginning, it would grow to great proportions and provide blessing and bounty for the many people who would come into it.

This new form of theocracy did begin with an insignificant beginning. Eleven men met in the upper room with Christ on the eve of His crucifixion. One hundred and twenty gathered to pray between His ascension and the descent of the Spirit on Pentecost. From such a small beginning the new form of the kingdom began to spread. In Acts 2 it increased to three thousand, and in Acts 4:4 the number was about five thousand. At the close of the Book of Acts it could be recorded that the whole world had heard the gospel (cf. Col. 1:6). This parable, then, was given to encourage the hearers to believe that the new form of the theocracy would grow to great proportions despite its insignificant beginning and despite Satan's opposition.

THE YEAST MIXED IN FLOUR
Matthew 13:33

THE PROBLEM

The parable of the weeds sown among the wheat (Matt. 13:24–30) raised the question of whether Satan can interrupt the progress of the kingdom. The answer is to be found in a study of the nature of yeast.

THE SOLUTION

Since bread was a staple of the diet in the Lord's day, the people would be very familiar with the reference made in this parable. Each day the housewife would grind wheat into flour. Then she would mix in with the flour a portion of dough retained from the previous day's bread making. The ingredients would then be set aside so that the yeast in the lump of dough from the previous day could do its work and cause the new dough to rise and be ready to be baked into bread. We are first introduced to yeast in the Scriptures in Exodus 12:8, 15–20 where the Israelites were told to leave all yeast behind when after the Passover they fled the land of bondage. Yeast represented continuity with the past. The Israelites knew nothing of yeast cakes with which they could bake bread. Instead, when some unbaked dough was ready for the oven, the housewife would set aside a portion of it to be used as yeast for the next day's mixture. This was done day by day so that the yeast provided an unbroken connection with the past. The Israelites were told to leave all yeast behind because they were to make a complete break with their previous servitude and were to enter into an entirely new life.

I vividly remember an illustration from my student days in seminary while ministering in a rural area in Texas. I was entertained for dinner at the home of an elderly man who had lived in that house for some seventy years. The host had been brought from Tennessee to Texas as a three-year-old child by his parents. At the meal we were served delicious hot bread. My host in-

58

formed me that this bread was made with yeast that his mother had brought from Tennessee some seventy years before. He took great pride in having kept that yeast alive for all those years. Further, he stated that the bread had been baked in a coal range and that the fire had been brought from the hearth his parents had left behind in Tennessee and that the fire had been kept burning for these seventy years. That yeast and that fire were a source of great pride to this elderly gentleman. He saw it as an unbroken connection with his heritage in the past.

Christ, then, was not using yeast to teach that the kingdom will be corrupted, for He had already explained to Nicodemus that only those who are born again can enter the kingdom. And Christ explained in later parables that not only is it true that the saved are in the kingdom now but they will have their part in the messianic form of the kingdom that is to come. Thus the emphasis is not on the nature of yeast that could represent evil but rather on the way that yeast works when it is once introduced into the mixture. When a housewife mixes yeast into the ingredients that will make bread, she starts a process that is irreversible and that will continue to work pervasively, persistently, and unseen until the entire mixture is made ready for the oven. The housewife has no way of interrupting or reversing the process when once it has begun.

Thus Christ in this simple figure was teaching that when the new form of the theocracy begins, it will work persistently, pervasively, and irreversibly. The sowing of the Word will produce irresistible growth. All earthly kingdoms have been established by military might. They have been established by the display of great external power. Christ taught that this new theocracy will be established, not by external power or discernible might, but rather by a quiet working from within.

THE TREASURE HIDDEN IN THE FIELD AND THE FINE PEARL
Matthew 13:44–45

THE PROBLEM

The Old Testament made it clear that God chose the nation of Israel to be His theocratic people through whom He would glorify Himself before the world (Ezek. 36:23–38). The question would then arise as to what would be accomplished through the new form of the theocracy. What benefit would accrue to God through the new form of the kingdom in this present age?

THE SOLUTION

Christ related two parables that provide an answer to this question. The problem in interpreting these two parables is to determine whether they are to be understood from a human viewpoint or from the divine viewpoint. If the man in the first parable and the merchant in the second represent individuals, then the parables are teaching the value of the kingdom and the desirability of entering it. In this interpretation the field in the first parable and the pearl in the second would be figures to represent the kingdom. The joy referred to in the first parable would be the recognition of the value of the kingdom. The selling in the two parables would represent the sacrifice made by the seeker in order to enter the kingdom. And the purchase in the two would represent the entrance into the kingdom. The lesson of the parables, then, would be that Christ's hearers should make every sacrifice necessary to enter the kingdom that He was offering them because of the benefit that would come to them from participation in the kingdom.

While this view is possible, it has a major difficulty in that it would seem to indicate that people enter the kingdom through their own sacrifice and by their own efforts. Since entrance into the kingdom is based on the new birth (John 3:5), this would teach a false doctrine of salvation. Therefore, it seems better to view the parables from a divine viewpoint. The man in the first and the merchant in the second would represent Christ Himself. The field in the first represents the world as it did in previous parables in this series. The purchase of the field and of the pearl refer to Christ's work on the cross to provide salvation for the sins of the whole world. We read, "He is the atoning sacrifice for our sins, and not only for ours but also for the sins of the whole world" (1 John 2:2) and "God was reconciling the world to himself in Christ, not counting men's sins against them" (2 Cor. 5:19). This purchase, then, provided the basis by which the new form of the theocracy would be established. Because of the purchase, the purchaser acquired a treasure and a fine pearl. These represent things of great value to the purchaser. The treasure hidden in the field may be a reference to a remnant from among Israel who will have their part in the new form of the kingdom. Thus Paul wrote that "at the present time there is a remnant [from Israel] chosen by grace" (Rom. 11:5). The pearl may be a reference to those from among the Gentiles who would have a part in this new form of the theocracy. Thus James said, "God at first showed his concern by taking from the Gentiles a people for himself" (Acts 15:14). This would provide the basis for Paul's doctrine when he wrote, "For he himself is our peace, who has made the two one and has destroyed the barrier, the dividing wall of hostility, by abolishing in his flesh the law with its commandments and regulations. His purpose was to create in himself one new man out of the two [Jew and Gentile], thus making peace, and in this one body to reconcile both of them to God through the cross, by which he put to death their hostility. He came and preached peace to you who were far away and peace to those who were near. For through him we both [Jew and Gentile] have access to the Father by one Spirit" (Eph. 2:14–18).

Thus these two parables revealed that through the program in the new form of the theocracy, Christ would purchase for Himself a special treasure made up of both Jews and Gentiles.

THE NET
Matthew 13:47–50

THE PROBLEM

Every previous form of the theocracy had ended in judgment: the expulsion from the Garden of Eden, the catastrophe of the Flood, the scattering from Babel, and the Exile. The question arose then of how this new form of the theocracy would end. The answer was given by Christ in the parable of the net.

THE SOLUTION

The normal way to fish on the Sea of Galilee was to stretch a net between two boats and then drag the net through the water. Later, the net would be drawn onto the shore. Since the net was indiscriminate in what it collected, the fishermen had to separate the edible from the inedible fish. The good fish were taken to market, and the inedible fish were cast away. This familiar practice was used by our Lord to picture what will happen at the end of the age. Jesus said people will be gathered by angelic instrumentality. The righteous will be received into the coming millennial theocracy, but the wicked will be excluded. No unsaved person will enter the Lord's millennial kingdom. The destiny of the wicked ultimately will be "the fiery furnace, where there will be weeping and gnashing of teeth" (Matt. 13:50). Jesus meant the wicked would be cast into "the lake of fire" (Rev. 20:14–15). The wicked, however, will not immediately be consigned to the lake of fire; intially, they will go into hades, evidently by experiencing physical death. The wicked will be detained in hades until they are resurrected for judgment before the Great White Throne (Rev. 20:11–15), after which they will be consigned to the lake of fire eternally. The parable, then, reveals that the present form of the theocracy will end with a judgment in which the wicked will be removed from the coming form of the kingdom. The righteous will be received into that millennial kingdom.

THE OWNER OF THE HOUSE
Matthew 13:52

THE PROBLEM

After Christ revealed the new form of the kingdom through parables, His hearers might well have asked what their responsibility was in the light of this truth that had been communicated. The Lord's answer was the parable of the owner of the house.

THE SOLUTION

Christ during the course of His earthly ministry often assumed the role of a rabbi and was frequently addressed as "Rabbi" (John 3:2 et al.). Those who heard Him teach "were amazed at his teaching, because he taught as one who had authority, and not as their teachers of the law" (Matt. 7:29). As a knowledgeable teacher He did what a wealthy person who had accumulated great stores did. Periodically, a wealthy person entered his storeroom and brought out things that could be distributed to those in need. A wealthy person may bring forth new wine or old wine, or new grain or old grain. The owner not only accumulated stores for personal use but for those for whom the owner was responsible. Christ was teaching that some features about this new form of the kingdom are similar to the previous forms of the kingdom while other aspects are new and unique. Examples of new aspects would be truths such as the universal proclamation of the kingdom, Satan's imitation of the kingdom, the outward growth of the kingdom, and the inner power of the kingdom. However, Christ's disclosures that the kingdom will include both Israel and the Gentiles and that the new form of the kingdom will end in judgment were similar to previous revelations concerning the theocracy and so would be old truths.

Since some from among the hearers would be administrators in the new form of the kingdom, Christ may have had them in mind as well since they were instructed in the new truths con-

63

cerning the new form of the kingdom. Their responsibility would be to share that knowledge the same way the owner of the storeroom shared his wealth with those for whom he was responsible.

THE WICKED SERVANT
Matthew 18:21–35

THE SETTING

In the prior context Christ had been asked, "Who is the greatest in the kingdom of heaven?" (Matt. 18:1). Using a child as an object lesson, He had responded, "Whoever humbles himself like this child is the greatest in the kingdom of heaven" (v. 4). In this oriental society a child had no rights; so Christ was saying that the one who gave up personal rights and submitted to His authority would have part in the kingdom of heaven. Christ warned the disciples against leading one of these little ones, that is, children of the kingdom, into sin (v. 6). Such little ones are objects of God's attention and are assigned angels to safeguard them (v. 10). Christ recognized that being in the family does not preclude misunderstandings and offenses, and He gave detailed instruction as to how differences should be resolved (vv. 15–17).

THE PROBLEM

The instruction concerning conflicts and misunderstandings raised a question in Peter's mind concerning one's obligation to forgive the offender. Peter knew that forgiveness was a characteristic of God and was to be exemplified in the righteous. Peter also knew that the Pharisees demanded forgiveness as an evidence of personal righteousness. The Pharisees required that one forgive the offender twice. Peter perhaps recalled that Christ had said, "If someone strikes you on the right cheek, turn to him the other also" (Matt. 5:39). Thus it would seem as though Christ's requirement was the same as that of the Pharisees. The Pharisees had added that if one wanted to go beyond what was required by the Pharisaic interpretation of the law, one should forgive three times. Therefore, Peter asked Christ, "Lord, how many times shall I forgive my brother when he sins against me? Up to seven times?" (18:21). Peter no doubt recalled that Christ had demanded that their righteousness should exceed the righteousness

65

of the teachers of the law and the Pharisees (5:20). And certainly seven times exceeded the demands of Pharisaism. Peter desired to know whether such forgiveness would be a demonstration of righteousness that satisfied Christ's demands.

THE SOLUTION

In order to answer Peter's question concerning the forgiveness that righteousness demands, Christ said that Peter should forgive "not seven times, but seventy-seven times" (Matt. 18:22). According to Jewish idiom "seventy-seven times" meant innumerable times. Thus Christ was saying righteousness demands that we forgive without keeping a record of the number of times forgiveness has been sought and granted. In order to further explain this truth, Christ told the parable of the wicked servant. In the parable a king called his servants to account. One owed him ten thousand talents. A talent was a measure of weight somewhere between sixty and eighty pounds. In today's money the amount owed by this servant would be several million dollars. Because the servant was not able to pay, the king commanded that the servant be sold into slavery to satisfy the debt which it was the king's right to do. However, since the price of a slave was thirty pieces of silver, the servant's enslavement could not possibly satisfy the indebtedness. Even though the servant had accumulated a debt that could not be repaid in a lifetime of labor, the servant asked for additional time. The king was under no obligation but was a merciful ruler; therefore he went beyond the servant's request and canceled the debt so that the servant left the king's presence free from all obligation.

Christ in His parable now presented the servant who had experienced such unlimited mercy as the creditor of a fellow servant who owed a hundred denarii, the equivalent of a few dollars. A denarius was a working person's wage for a day's labor. Such a debt could be discharged through the frugality and diligence of the debtor. After the creditor demanded immediate repayment, the debtor asked for additional time with a promise to pay the debt. However, the creditor threw the debtor into prison until the debt could be paid. The lack of mercy shown to the creditor was conveyed to the king by the debtor's friends. And in response the forgiven debtor was called into the presence of the king, who said, "I canceled all that debt of yours because you begged me to. Shouldn't you have had mercy on your fellow servant just as I had on you?" (Matt. 18:32–33).

It is in the response of the king to the lack of mercy of the wicked servant that we find Christ's answer to Peter's question. The forgiven servant was responsible to forgive debtors in the same measure that the king had extended forgiveness. Since mercy had been extended to the servant, that servant was responsible as a creditor to extend mercy to debtors who sought forgiveness. Since we by nature are sinners, we have accumulated a debt that we are incapable of paying. Christ in mercy provided a salvation for sinners. And the one who seeks God's forgiveness through Jesus Christ is mercifully forgiven all debts. No one can measure one's indebtedness to God for the forgiveness God has granted. Therefore, there should be no measure to the forgiveness that we grant those who seek forgiveness from us.

The latter part of the parable has disturbed many, for at first glance it appears that Christ might be teaching that if we have received God's forgiveness and then fail to forgive, we will lose our salvation. However, Christ actually was teaching that one who does not forgive is giving evidence of not having received forgiveness from God and therefore must be removed from God's presence.

THE GOOD SHEPHERD
John 10:1–18

THE SETTING

Isaiah, picturing the coming Messiah, wrote, "See, the sovereign LORD comes with power, and his arm rules for him. See, his reward is with him, and his recompense accompanies him. He tends his flock like a shepherd: He gathers the lambs in his arms and carries them close to his heart; he gently leads those that are with young" (Isa. 40:10–11). Offering Himself to Israel as the Messiah, Christ claimed to be the Shepherd of Israel, who will lead His flock into green pastures and beside still waters. Christ gave evidence through both His words and works that He was the covenanted and prophesied Messiah. The nation became engulfed in a debate over His person. The leaders of the nation were adamant in their decision that He was not who He claimed to be but rather was a blasphemous imposter who received power from Satan, not from God.

THE PROBLEM

In John 9 Christ had performed the notable miracle of healing a man born blind. By healing the man's physical blindness, Christ was indicating to Israel that He was the One who could remove their spiritual blindness (cf. John 9:35–38). This miracle raised the question of the identity of the person of Christ. Who was He? Was He truly the Messiah? Our Lord answered this question through His parabolic use of the shepherd and his sheep.

THE SOLUTION

Sheepfolds were walled enclosures built either of stone or of thorny hedge and were provided with a narrow entrance. The enclosure was a place of refuge and protection for the flock in times of danger or in the event of inclement weather. A number of flocks would be given refuge in a single sheepfold. The door to

68

the sheepfold would be secured and watched over by a watchman. When the danger had passed, the shepherd would approach the gate and the watchman would open it. Then the shepherd would stand at the door and call his sheep. Since a shepherd's sheep could recognize his voice, the animals would separate themselves from the many flocks that had been secured in the sheepfold. They would follow their own shepherd out of the fold to pasture and water.

Using this familiar imagery, Christ first demonstrated that He was the true Shepherd. He had entered the sheepfold by the gate, that is, in the appointed way. If He had been a thief who sought to lead away another's sheep, He would have sought access to the sheep in some way other than by coming to the gate to identify Himself to the watchman. In the imagery here, Christ used the sheepfold to represent the nation of Israel. But there were many in Israel who called themselves shepherds who were in fact false shepherds. This had been predicted by Zechariah when he said, "Then the LORD said to me, 'Take again the equipment of a foolish shepherd. For I am going to raise up a shepherd over the land who will not care for the lost or seek the young, or heal the injured, or feed the healthy, but will eat the meat of the choice sheep, tearing off their hoofs'" (11:15–16). In the imagery of the parable, John the Baptist was represented as a watchman whose ministry was to introduce Christ to the nation of Israel in accordance with prophecy (Mal. 3:1). John fulfilled this ministry and introduced Christ to the nation (Matt. 3:2; John 1:29) as both the Savior and the Sovereign. Christ is to be identified as the true Shepherd, for He came in accordance with the prophecies describing His coming. He was born of a virgin (Isa. 7:14; Matt. 1:22–23). He was born in Bethlehem (Mic. 5:2; Luke 2:4–7). He was born in David's line (2 Sam. 7:16; Matt. 1:1–17; Luke 3:23–37). Examples could be multiplied to show that every prophecy spoken in the Old Testament concerning the person and the work of Christ at His first advent has been fulfilled. The fulfillment of prophecy shows that He is the true Shepherd. But, contrariwise, not one of the Pharisees who claimed to be a shepherd and who sought authority over the flock could give such proof.

A second proof that He was who He claimed to be is that those who are His own sheep listen to His voice and recognize Him and are willing to follow Him (John 10:3–4). The entire flock, that is, the nation of Israel, did not recognize and accept Him at His first advent, but a small remnant did place faith in Him and acknowledged that He is the true Shepherd; and individual Jews have continued to trust Him. In these ways, then, Christ in this parabolic discourse answered the question as to who He was.

This leads to a second question; namely, what kind of Shepherd is He? In "I am the gate; whoever enters through me will be saved" (John 10:9), He thus is the Shepherd who provides salvation. Further, He also is the Shepherd who liberates, for His sheep "will come in and go out." This emphasizes the liberty or freedom that He provides. In addition, He is a Shepherd who satisfies. His own sheep shall "find pasture," for He has "come that they may have life, and have it to the full" (vv. 8–10). Moreover, He is the Shepherd who "lays down his life for the sheep" (vv. 11, 15, 18). This shows that this Shepherd's care is not for Himself but for the sheep. These are characteristics of Christ as a Shepherd that no false shepherd could claim to possess. These characteristics of Christ as a Shepherd give further proof that He is what He claimed to be—the true Shepherd of Israel.

THE GOOD SAMARITAN
Luke 10:30–37

THE SETTING

The nation of Israel was fully aware through both the words and works of Jesus Christ that He was offering Himself to Israel as their Messiah and presenting the promised and covenanted Davidic kingdom. The Old Testament had made it very clear that righteousness was a prerequisite for entrance into that kingdom. The people were sufficiently convinced by the evidence that Christ gave of the genuineness of His offer that they began to concern themselves with questions of righteousness. It must have been widely known that Christ repudiated the righteousness of the Pharisees as providing an acceptable basis for entrance into His kingdom (Matt. 5:20). Instead of Pharisaic righteousness Christ demanded perfection; He had said, "Be perfect, therefore, as your heavenly Father is perfect" (Matt. 5:48). Scholars of the Mosaic law frequently came to Christ to ask His interpretation of the law and to discuss His concept of righteousness.

THE PROBLEM

Two related questions were asked by the expert in the law in the context immediately preceding the parable of the good Samaritan. The questions occur in Luke 10:25 and 29, and both probed Christ as to His concept of the righteousness that would please a holy God.

THE SOLUTION

The expert in the law addressed Christ as "Teacher" (Luke 10:25). By so addressing Christ this law expert recognized Him as a scholar in the law and showed that he desired to discuss Christ's interpretation of the righteousness of the law. His first question was "What must I do to inherit eternal life?" (v. 25). This question has been much misunderstood and has been used to suggest that

71

salvation may be obtained by works. Such is contrary to the whole tenor of Scripture. Paul said, "For when the kindness and love of God our Savior appeared, he saved us, not because of righteous things we had done, but because of his mercy. He saved us through the washing of rebirth and renewal by the Holy Spirit, whom he poured out on us generously through Jesus Christ our Savior, so that, having been justified by his grace, we might become heirs having the hope of eternal life" (Titus 3:4–7). Paul added, "For it is by grace you have been saved, through faith— and this not from yourselves, it is the gift of God—not by works, so that no one can boast" (Eph. 2:8–9). This faith principle not only was clearly enunciated in the New Testament but also was true in the Old Testament, for Paul wrote, "We, too, have put our faith in Christ Jesus that we may be justified by faith in Christ and not by observing the law, because by observing the law no one will be justified" (Gal. 2:16–17). It must be realized that in Jewish thinking entrance into the messianic kingdom was equated with inheriting eternal life. The millennial kingdom was the stepping stone to the eternal kingdom. One who was in the millennial kingdom would be in the eternal kingdom. Thus to enter the millennial kingdom was to enter into eternal life.

The question of the law expert in Luke 10:25, then, must be understood to mean, "How righteous must I be to enter the messianic kingdom that You are offering? Or, What right- eousnesses must I show in my life to demonstrate that I am righteous to the degree that renders me eligible to enter the king- dom?"

Scripture teaches that while works do not produce righteous- ness, righteousness will produce works. This was James' point when he said, "What good is it, my brothers, if a man claims to have faith but has no deeds? Can such faith save him? . . . Faith by itself, if it is not accompanied by action, is dead. . . . I will show you my faith by what I do" (James 2:14, 17–18). We must not understand from the man's question in Luke 10:25 that he was asking what he could do to be saved, for such a wrong understanding will cause us to misunderstand Christ when He replied, "What is written in the Law? . . . How do you read it? . . . Do this and you will live" (vv. 26–28). Christ was not telling the man that he would be saved by keeping the law. The man wanted to know how righteous he must be in order to enter the kingdom and what works he could do to prove that he had been made righteous. Christ in replying to his interrogation used the law lawfully. The law was primarily designed to be a revelation of the holiness of God (1 Peter 1:15–16). It also revealed the demands that God made of those who wished to be acceptable to Him and to walk in fellowship with Him (Matt. 5:48). This scholar in the law could examine the law and from the law would know that God is holy. Further, this law expert could know the demands that God's holiness would make on those who desired to be in fellowship with Him—on those who wished to be admitted to Messiah's kingdom.

That the man was thoroughly conversant with the law was evident in his response to Christ's question concerning what the law demanded: "'Love the Lord your God with all your heart and with all your soul and with all your strength and with all your mind'; and, 'Love your neighbor as yourself'" (Luke 10:27). He was quoting Deuteronomy 6:5 and Leviticus 19:18. Christ, who approved the man's answer, similarly summarized the demands of the law (Matt. 22:36–40).

It is readily evident that that knowledge did not satisfy. The man's knowledge only brought conviction, for he sought to "justify himself" (Luke 10:29). This makes it clear that the man stood convicted by the knowledge of his failure to produce the fruits of righteousness that would admit him into Messiah's kingdom. His defense was his ignorance. He asked, "Who is my neighbor?" He thus implied that he was not at fault for not presenting these proofs of his righteousness; rather, the fault was in the law. The law, he claimed, did not make it clear who his neighbor was. Thus the man was inferring that if he had known who his neighbor was, he would have fulfilled the requirement of the law. This question clearly reveals that the man stood convicted by the law that he knew. This raised the second question (Luke 10:29), and

Christ in His ingenious way sought to answer it as well as the previous question (v. 25) through the parable of the Good Samaritan.

Jericho is about twelve miles northeast of Jerusalem and is located in the depths of the Jordan Valley. Between the two cities was the desert of Judea, a rocky wasteland infested with bandits. People usually sought to travel in groups for protection from the robbers. This lone man had been set on by robbers, who had beaten him mercilessly, robbed him of all he possessed—even his clothing—and left him in his helpless state alongside the road. Christ now introduced three who had traveled the same road. The first two were among the religious leaders of Israel—a priest and a Levite. Since Jericho was a resident city for priests and Levites, these may well have been returning from ministries in the temple. When these two saw the man, they must have immediately recognized his need. Because of the position that religious leaders held in the nation, they would have been men of above-average wealth and would have been able to meet the need. But both in turn, even though seeing the need and being able to meet it, refused to respond. Christ in this part of the parable was answering the question, "Who is my neighbor?" The Lord's answer shows that our neighbor is any person in need whose need we know and whose need we are able to meet. If we refuse to respond to the need, then we are not neighborly. Christ was answering the question negatively in this part of the parable. He then proceeded to answer the question positively. The third traveler was a Samaritan—one who was considered an outcast by the Jews (John 4:9). When the Samaritan saw the injured man, "he took pity on him" (Luke 10:33). He was moved with compassion. He immediately responded to the need according to his ability. He had on hand oil to soothe and wine to cleanse, and he poured these on the man's injuries and also bandaged them. Because it was impossible for the injured man to be properly cared for where he was, the Samaritan put him on his own donkey, transported him to an inn, and entrusted him to the care of the innkeeper. The Samaritan paid for the man's keep, promising the innkeeper that when he returned he would make a full reimbursement for any extra cost that had been involved.

Christ thus answered the question, "Who is my neighbor?" by saying that any person whose need we know and whose need we are able to meet is our neighbor. We fulfill the righteousness of the law that demands that we love our neighbor as ourselves when we respond to such a person's need according to our ability.

Thus Christ was explaining what the law demanded when it required love for one's neighbor as an evidence of true righteousness. The lesson was so clear that when Christ asked His interrogator who of the three was fulfilling the law, the questioner responded, "The one who had mercy on him" (Luke 10:37). The teacher of the law had no further excuse for pleading ignorance regarding the righteousness that the law demanded. Christ then concluded His discourse, saying, "Go and do likewise." Again, many have misunderstood Christ to be teaching that one can enter the kingdom or receive salvation on the basis of what one does. However, when the original question "What must I do to inherit eternal life?" (v. 25) is understood to be an inquiry by the law expert concerning what kind of righteousness he must show to be admitted into the kingdom, then Christ's answer is very clear. If this man was to prove himself righteous, he must show mercy to others as he had been shown mercy by the God whose forgiveness he had sought and received. Since Christ was considered to be a Samaritan by the religious leaders (John 8:48), He through the parable may have been showing the man the way to obtain the righteousness that he confessed was necessary for entrance into the kingdom. Righteousness does not come through works but through the mercy of the rejected One who saw the sinner's need and responded to that need by the sacrifice of Himself.

THE PERSISTENT FRIEND
Luke 11:1–10

THE SETTING

The Pharisees set great store by prayer. Following the example of Daniel (cf. Dan. 6:10), they prayed three times during the course of the day—at the third hour, the sixth hour, and the ninth hour. The Pharisees did their praying in public (Luke 18:10–11). Instead of uttering prayers as petitions to God, the Pharisees sought to impress people with their piety. Christ deemed such prayer to be hypocritical, for He said, "They love to pray standing in the synagogues and on the street corners to be seen by men. I tell you the truth, they have received their reward in full" (Matt. 6:5). The praying of the Pharisees was deemed by Christ to be babbling and as such was not on any higher level than the empty repetition of pagans (v. 7). Those following the pattern of the Pharisees had never learned to pray.

The preaching of John the Baptist had been believed by many Jews who were anticipating the coming of the Messiah. Since prayer is a vital link between the believer and God, John had taught his disciples to pray (Luke 5:33).

THE PROBLEM

Many of John's disciples had turned from him to follow Jesus and would have known how to pray. However, there were evidently many who had not received John's instructions, and in the minds of these was the question of how they should pray. Therefore, they came to Christ, asking, "Lord, teach us to pray" (Luke 11:1).

THE SOLUTION

Christ began His response by giving them a model of prayer. This was not a prayer to be repeated ritually but rather one that stressed the areas in which a believer ought to be concerned while praying. Prayer, first, will be addressed to our "Father." This title

76

signifies a relationship that has been established by faith. Prayer concerns itself with worship, as indicated by the words "hallowed be your name." Prayer also occupies itself with God's work, for Jesus added, "Your kingdom come." Then too prayer rightfully petitions God for personal needs, as the clause "Give us each day our daily bread" shows. Again, prayer concerns itself with forgiveness and restoration; thus Jesus continued, "Forgive us our sins." It is expected that a righteous God will forgive sins when we ask because one of the evidences of righteousness is the forgiveness of others. If righteousness demands forgiveness, certainly a righteous God may be petitioned for forgiveness. Finally, prayer seeks protection from the evil one; Jesus said, "Lead us not into temptation." All of these are areas of daily concern. To safeguard His hearers against the error of thinking that repetition in prayer until the need is met falls into the category of "babbling" (Matt. 6:7), Christ told the parable that follows. In it He emphasized one particular kind of prayer—intercession.

People normally traveled only during the daylight hours because of the dangers that could befall them after dark. If at nightfall the destination had not been reached, the traveler would seek refuge in an inn where one could safely spend the night and then continue the journey the next day. In the parable a traveler had violated the normal custom and had continued on the journey to a friend's house until midnight. The traveler would have been exhausted and hungry after such a long journey, and hospitality would have demanded that the traveler be provided both food and shelter. While the host could provide shelter, there was no food in the house to offer the traveler. The host recognized the need for food and felt responsible to meet that need too. Since the host had a friend who could meet the need for the food, the host braved the dangers of the dark and went to the friend's house to intercede in behalf of the needy guest. However, the host met with refusal after knocking at the door of the friend's house. In biblical times houses were very small, often with only one room; that room served as a living room for the family by day but became the family bedroom at night. For one to arise and light the lamp and admit a guest into the house required that the entire family arise and extend hospitality to the visitor. This the friend was unwilling to do. The intercessor, because he recognized the need of the guest, persisted in his asking. The host continued to ask until the friend obliged. It was not the need that moved the friend, nor friendship with the intercessor, but rather the persistence of the intercessor that brought a response. Jesus pointed out, "Though he will not get up and give him the bread because he is his friend, yet because of the man's persistence he will get up and give him as much as he needs" (Luke 11:8).

Christ by this parable was teaching that when a person recognizes a need that he or she is personally unable to meet, that person is placed in the role of an intercessor. The believer has an obligation to persist in the ministry of intercession until the thing has been provided that will meet the need. Christ was not inferring that God is unwilling to hear, for we know that "his ears are attentive" to the prayers of the righteous (1 Peter 3:12). Christ was teaching here by contrast. If even an unwilling human friend can be moved by persistent intercession, how much more will God be moved by the persistence of an intercessor!

Christ applied the truth of the parable in Luke 11:9–10, where the Greek reads literally as follows: "Keep on asking and it will be given to you; keep on seeking and you will find; keep on knocking and the door will be opened to you. For everyone who keeps on asking receives; he who keeps on seeking finds; and to him who keeps on knocking, the door will be opened." Persistent intercession is not the babbling of the heathen. It is a manifestation of one's faith in the faithfulness of God, who in His own time will respond to the need of the one for whom we have become an intercessor. An intercessor, then, is a go-between between one in need and the One who can meet that need, and persistence on the part of the intercessor is required until that need is met.

THE RICH FOOL
Luke 12:16–21

THE SETTING

Christ in Luke 12 warned the vast multitude that assembled to hear Him teach concerning the pervasive attitude that characterized the Pharisees. In verses 1–11 He dealt with hypocrisy and in verses 13–34 with covetousness. The question of covetousness was brought up by the challenge thrown at Christ by one from the multitude, who requested, "Teacher, tell my brother to divide the inheritance with me" (v. 13). Christ had been offering Himself to the nation as their Messiah, and Psalm 72:2 states that one of the roles of Messiah was to act as an arbiter: "He will judge your people in righteousness, your afflicted ones with justice." The challenger, knowing the claims of Christ, asked for a demonstration of Messiah's right to judge. At first glance Christ's reply seems to deny that He would be an Arbiter, for He said, "Man, who appointed me a judge or an arbiter between you?" (Luke 12:14). However, Christ was not denying that when He rules as Messiah, He will serve as a Judge. The reason He spoke to the multitude as He did was that the nation had rejected him as Messiah; therefore, He had no right to impose His decisions on them. Only the nation's voluntary submission to Him as their Judge will make it possible for Him to exercise judgment. Thus Christ recognized the man's challenge as an evidence of unbelief, not faith in His person.

THE PROBLEM

The Pharisees set great store by material possessions. In Deuteronomy 28 God promised material blessings for obedience. Material possessions, then, were viewed as a sign of God's good pleasure in the person who possessed them. The pursuit of material possessions became the highest goal in life in order that, by having many possessions, one could give public evidence of being approved by God. The prevailing Jewish attitude toward

79

possessions was expressed in the statement "Whom the lord loveth, He maketh rich." If God's blessing was to be sought, then riches—the sign of that blessing—should eagerly be pursued. The following questions then arose: What is wrong with the pursuit of material possessions? Why is covetousness or greed to be shunned?

THE SOLUTION

In order to answer this problem, Christ told the parable of the rich fool. It is to be noted that at the start of the parable the farmer was already rich (Luke 12:16). The man had not become rich by the new harvest. Instead, the harvest only added to his riches. Before the new harvest, this rich man already had barns filled to capacity. He did not need the added wealth to sustain himself or his household.

When the new harvest came and the rich farmer realized that he had no place to store the crop, his solution was "I will tear down my barns and build bigger ones, and there I will store all my grain and my goods" (Luke 12:18). This solution to the problem of the man's increased wealth shows that he had no concern for his neighbor. There were many poor people. The man had a great opportunity to show his righteousness by fulfilling the second requirement of the law by distributing his excess wealth to those in need. However, this never seems to have entered his mind. Thus the man demonstrated that he was not righteous when tested by the requirements of the law.

The man in addition showed that he did not fulfill the first requirement of the law, that is, "Love the Lord your God with all your heart and with all your soul and with all your strength and with all your mind" (Luke 10:27). He said to himself, "You have plenty of good things laid up for many years. Take life easy; eat, drink and be merry" (12:19). He was showing that his first love was for himself and his own comfort and enjoyment. Thus he was not righteous before the first great commandment of the law. He was showing that his primary goal in life was to satisfy himself and to use for his own selfish purposes the wealth that he had accumulated. This leads to the observation that in Scripture a person is not considered rich merely because he has material possessions. The rich are those who *trust* in riches, use them for selfish ends, and are thus ungrateful to God who provided salvation through faith and trust in Jesus Christ. The rich person, then, is not determined by the amount of possessions, but rather by his or her attitude toward those possessions. It was not the possessions or acquisition of possessions that Christ was here condemning but rather the attitude toward those possessions that characterized the rich man in the parable. The man was covetous because he sought to acquire goods for his own selfish ends, and he was greedy because he misused the possessions that he had acquired. Christ now proceeded in the parable to answer the question and to show that the folly of covetousness and greed leads to the selfish accumulation of material goods. While the man considered himself to be sovereign over his possessions, the parable moves on to show that God was sovereign over the man's life. The man was pronounced by God to be a fool (Luke 12:20). According to Scripture, a fool is a man who leaves God out of any consideration. Thus, Psalm 141:1 says, "The fool says in his heart, 'There is no God.'" This man was a fool in that he did not recognize his material blessings as coming from God, nor did he recognize any obligation to God in the use of his possessions. As a judgment for his helplessness, God said, "This very night your life will be demanded from you" (Luke 12:20a). The Creator is sovereign over the creature, and the creature is answerable to the Creator. Christ was emphasizing that any individual is responsible to God for the use of all that he possesses. God asked, "Then who will get what you have prepared for yourself?" (Luke 12:20b). Christ was thus emphasizing that possessions are temporal, not eternal. It was impossible for the man to use material possessions in the place where he was going. Material things are designed for this life, not for the life to come. Therefore, the man was investing his whole life in what was temporary, not in what is eternal. Christ drew an application from this principle, stating, "This is how it will be with anyone who stores up things for himself but is not rich toward God" (Luke 12:21). Christ was showing that although material possessions are considered temporary, they may be used to acquire eternal riches. The man had had abundant opportunity to use his material possessions unselfishly and thus demonstrate that he was righteous and consequently assured of eternal reward. However, by his greed, covetousness, and selfishness, he demonstrated that he was unrighteous and hence would not acquire eternal reward.

Fools leave God out of their lives and have no one but themselves in whom to trust. They must therefore make provision for themselves, both for today and tomorrow. The alternative is to be wise and trust God. Christ applied the principle of this parable by showing that one cannot adequately supply for oneself by taking concern for oneself. The alternative is to trust God, who feeds the ravens and clothes the lilies. Christ gave the promise, "If that is how God clothes the grass of the field, which is here today, and tomorrow is thrown into the fire, how much more will he clothe you, you of little faith!" (Luke 12:28). Believers should not set their hearts on the accumulation of riches and trust riches; instead, they should trust the heavenly Father. Christ's counsel was "Do not set your heart on what you will eat or drink; do not worry about it. . . . But seek his kingdom, and these things will be given to you as well" (vv. 29–31). We need not covet riches to provide security, for we have a Father who has promised to care for us. If we trust the Father, we will accumulate "a treasure in heaven that will not be exhausted, where no thief comes near and no moth destroys" (v. 33).

THE FAITHFUL SERVANTS
Luke 12:35–40

THE SETTING

Because of Israel's evident rejection of Him as the Messiah and the postponement of His millennial kingdom until the Second Advent, Christ was giving instruction to His disciples to whom the ministry would be committed following His death. Christ gave much of this instruction to them in parables.

THE PROBLEM

Several related questions would quite naturally arise in the minds of Christ's hearers when they recognized that they would be commissioned as servants during His absence. They would wonder what He would expect of them. What are the characteristics of a true servant, and what rewards may a true servant expect?

THE SOLUTION

In two brief parables the Lord gave the characteristics of a true servant. As He frequently did the Lord used the imagery of a wedding banquet. Such a banquet was of indeterminate length. The banquet might consist only of a single meal; but if the host were a person of wealth, the feasting could continue for days. When the master of the servants attended a wedding banquet, he would be absent from the household for an indeterminate length of time. Because of the uncertainty a servant might neglect normal responsibilities and become lazy. Such a servant would be faithless. On the other hand a servant might diligently attend to the usual duties regardless of the master's absence and the uncertainty of the time of the master's return. A servant's responsibilities included tending the gate and opening the gate for the returning master. A faithless servant, counting on a long delay, would leave the gate unattended. However, a faithful servant would be unaffected by the uncertainties and delay and would

83

diligently be on duty when the master returned. Thus the Lord was teaching that a faithful servant performs the assigned task; such a servant is not affected by the master's absence and the possible delay of the master's return.

Having exhorted His disciples to be faithful, Christ enlarged on the simile of a wedding banquet. The Lord said the reward to be given to faithful servants is great. The master has them "recline at the table" and will come and wait on them (Luke 12:37). Thus the faithful servant will be served, and his faithfulness will be the basis of reward when the master returns.

There would seem to be no legitimate reason to neglect one's diligent attendance to duty. Since it was not customary to travel at night, a servant might conclude as night fell that the master would not be coming before morning. The servant might reason further that this was a legitimate circumstance in which to neglect a duty. However, the Lord said that in spite of this, the servant should remain on duty and be found faithful. The master could come "in the second or third watch of the night" (Luke 12:38). The second watch was the three hours before midnight and the third watch was the three hours after midnight. Thus we see that the Lord gave no excuse for unfaithfulness, no matter how reasonable the excuse might appear to be.

The Lord enlarged on this concept in an additional parable. The owner of the house was not only the provider for the household but also the protector. His responsibility was to see that servants were assigned to stand guard at the gate that provided the only access by which a thief might enter a household to rob it. The gate normally was guarded under all circumstances; but certainly if the owner were forewarned of the time of the approach of a thief, that owner would secure the gates with additional guards to protect the members of the household. One would be derelict in one's responsibility to the household if one did not secure the gate with sufficient guards to protect it.

Christ in this brief parable was emphasizing the responsibility that rests on servants. Their responsibility is to safeguard what has been entrusted to their care. If they do not protect what is entrusted to them, they are unfaithful servants. Servants must guard their stewardship. By this Christ was preparing His disciples for the attacks that Satan would make against them and against their ministry (cf. John 15:18–16:4).

These parables were designed to instruct the disciples concerning faithfulness in the ministry entrusted to them in view of the fact that at the time of the Lord's return they will have to give an account of their stewardship. Since the coming of Christ is promised but the time of His coming is indeterminate, Christ's disciples are required to be faithful constantly, lest at His coming they be found unfaithful.

THE FRUITLESS FIG TREE
Luke 13:6–9

Some people approached Christ with a problem that was both political and religious in nature. They referred to an atrocity perpetrated by Pilate in which some Galileans had been murdered. This raised a religious problem in the minds of the interrogators because according to Pharisaic theology, every tragedy was seen as a divine penalty for some sin. These desired to know what sin would have been so heinous in the sight of God that it brought about such a retribution. The purpose of this question may have been to discredit Christ, who affirmed that He had come to reveal God to them. It would seem to the natural mind that no sin could merit such an atrocity; and if this murder had come from God, then such a God would not merit obedience or worship.

The second issue was political, and it is possible that this question was a carefully planned attempt to discredit Christ as a Teacher. If in order to defend the character of God, He attributed this atrocity to Pilate and condemned Pilate for its perpetration, then He would seem to be guilty of treason.

By His answer Christ sought to correct the false doctrine of the Pharisees that attributed all natural calamities to a divine judgment. If such were true, then Pilate would have killed all the Galileans because all of them were sinners. In order to support His argument Christ made a historical reference to eighteen people who lost their lives when the tower in Siloam fell on them while they were engaged in the work of construction. Pharisees would have attributed their deaths to divine judgment. Christ said if that were true, then all in Jerusalem would have had to perish because all were sinners in the sight of God.

Christ then made the application that those who had broached the question were sinners needing to repent. His questioners doubtless followed the doctrines of the Pharisees and consequently considered themselves to be righteous. The fact that they had not come under judgment would seem to validate their righteousness, but Christ passed judgment on them while also inviting them to repent in order to escape the coming judgment.

THE PROBLEM

With the announcement that the judgment would come on those who deemed themselves righteous unless they repented, the question arose as to why this judgment would come. Christ gave the answer in the parable of the fruitless fig tree.

THE SOLUTION

The owner of a vineyard had planted a fig tree. This tree was not planted for ornamentation or firewood but for fruit. While the owner did not expect fruit the first year, certainly by the second and third years the owner could anticipate an abundance of fruit. The figure of the fig tree in this parable conveyed the same truth that Isaiah taught through the use of the vine in Isaiah 5:1–7, explaining, "The vineyard of the LORD Almighty is the house of Israel, and the men of Judah are the garden of his delight. And he looked for justice, but saw bloodshed; for righteousness, but heard cries of distress" (v. 7). God desired to see righteousness and justice in the people whom He had chosen to be instruments for His glory. After sufficient time had passed for the tree to mature, the owner approached the one who cared for the vineyard. The owner expected to receive fruit from the tree, but no fruit had been gathered. In this parable the man who took care of the vineyard is a figure of God Himself. God had entered into a covenant with the nation of Israel and had entrusted the care of the nation to the One who had come as Israel's Messiah. Like His predecessor the Messiah has called them to repentance and exhorted them to produce the fruits of righteousness. But the nation had not responded. In the parable the owner of the vineyard passed judgment on the unproductive tree. He said, "Cut it down! Why should it use up the soil?" (Luke 13:7). The fig tree proved by a long period of unproductiveness that it was a permanently barren tree and consequently was worthless; moreover, it took up space where a fruitful tree might be planted.

Therefore judgment was passed. The parable does not mean that divine judgment will terminate the nation as a covenant people; rather the parable means that God announced judgment on a generation that had proved itself fruitless.

At this point the one to whose care the fig tree had been entrusted interceded for the tree. he asked, "Leave it alone for one more year, and I'll dig around it and fertilize it. If it bears fruit next year, fine! If not, then cut it down" (Luke 13:8). Judgment might well have fallen on that generation and Christ could have continued His program with the small remnant that believed on Him. From them Christ might have gathered the fruits of righteousness that would have pleased the One who had made Him Custodian of the nation. However, He interceded with the Judge, asking that judgment be postponed for a brief period to permit Him to continue His work of tending the tree so that, if possible, it might become a fruitful tree. The Messiah did not want the fruitlessness to be attributed to His neglect, and so He asked for an opportunity to give further attention to the fruitless tree. The fact that judgment did not fall on the nation of Israel at that time, but was ultimately postponed until A.D. 70, when Titus overthrew Jerusalem, suggests that the Intercessor's petition was granted and that the period leading up to that judgment provided Israel an opportunity to prove themselves a fruitful tree. The fact that judgment did fall shows that no fruit of righteousness was produced by the nation of Israel.

SEATS AT A WEDDING FEAST
Luke 14:7–11

THE SETTING

The culture of Christ's day set great store by hospitality. A host would invite guests to dine in order to be honored by the guests, and the guests welcomed an invitation to join in a meal as an opportunity to be honored. The motivation in extending hospitality was not to fulfill the righteousness of the law but rather to accumulate honor for either the host or the guest. The banquets provided an opportunity for a lavish display of one's wealth, and the guests enjoyed what was lavished on them.

THE PROBLEM

Since hospitality—a demonstration of unselfish compassion —was so perverted from what God intended it to be, the following question arose: With what attitude should one respond to an invitation to attend a wedding banquet?

THE SOLUTION

The reason Christ spoke this parable on this occasion was because "he noticed how the guests picked the places of honor at the table" (Luke 14:7). It was an honor in itself just to be invited to a wedding feast; however, those invited sought even greater honor for themselves by claiming the seats of honor at the banquet. Such seats were at the right hand or the left hand of the host, and the host had the right to assign these places of honor. The guests whom Christ mentioned on this occasion had not waited for the host to assign them to their respective places; instead, they had chosen places of high honor for themselves. They were measuring themselves by themselves, and they deemed themselves to be superior to all others.

In order to correct this unrighteous attitude, Christ instructed the guests that they were not to take the places of honor at the

89

right hand or the left hand of the host, for the host did not need to abide by their claim to be the most honorable among the guests. The host might exercise his right and remove the persons from the seats that they had assumed. He could then humiliate them publicly by consigning them seats at the end of the table that would have been in the least significant place. It would indeed have been humiliating to the guests who sought the seats of honor to have it revealed that the host did not judge them as they had judged themselves. Instead of humiliating them, Christ instructed them. He said they should assume that the others were all superior to themselves and worthy of more honor. Instead of taking the seats of honor, they should take the lowest places. The host was the last to arrive at the banquet. Having put in an appearance and having surveyed the guests, the host had a right to honor those who had taken the lowest place and to invite them to "move up to a better place" (Luke 14:10). Thus these would be honored before all of the other guests. True honor is not the honor that one claims for oneself, but rather it is the honor that is conferred on one by others. Christ's application was very clear when He said, "For everyone who exalts himself will be humbled, and he who humbles himself will be exalted" (v. 11).

Christ not only corrected the wrong attitude of the guests who approached the banquet, but He also corrected the wrong attitude of the host. Having addressed the guests, Christ told the host not to use hospitality as a means of bringing honor to oneself by inviting friends, relatives, or rich neighbors. Instead, the host should invite the poor, the crippled, the lame, and the blind. The friends, relatives, and rich neighbors could requite the host by returning the invitation and offering an even more lavish banquet than that the host had provided. The poor, the crippled, the lame, and the blind were incapable of repaying the host. The ability to provide a banquet and the opportunity to extend hospitality were not to be used for self-aggrandizement. Rather, these were means by which the righteousness of the law might be displayed in that the one providing the banquet recognized the needs of others and invited the needy to the banquet. While the host would have no honor from the guests, the righteousness of the host would be recognized by God and the host would be "repaid at the resurrection of the righteous" (Luke 14:14). Thus Christ was saying that it is preferable to seek honor from God than from people.

THE GREAT BANQUET
Luke 14:16–24

THE SETTING

The figure of a banquet or a wedding feast was frequently used by our Lord to represent Israel's millennial kingdom. In that kingdom the King would make a bountiful provision for all the subjects of His kingdom. There would be no famine, poverty, hunger, or want. This bounty was pictured by the prophet Amos, who said, "'The days are coming,' declares the LORD, 'when the reaper will be overtaken by the plowman and the planter by the one treading grapes. New wine will drip from the mountains and flow from all the hills. I will bring back my exiled people from Israel; they will rebuild the ruined cities and live in them. They will plant vineyards and drink their wine; they will make gardens and eat their fruit'" (9:13–14). In the previous parable Christ's use of the figure of a marriage feast had brought to the minds of His hearers the prophetic picture of Israel's millennial kingdom. One of those around the banquet table where Christ had delivered His rebuke burst out, "Blessed is the man who will eat at the feast in the kingdom of God" (Luke 14:15).

THE PROBLEM

As no one preparing a banquet invited everyone in the community to attend, the question arose as to who would be in attendance at the millennial banquet that Messiah would spread.

THE SOLUTION

Continuing to use the figure of the marriage banquet, Christ told of a man who had prepared a great banquet. According to the custom, the betrothal would have taken place some twelve months before the actual wedding and its consequent banquet. Thus a year had now elapsed since the invitation had been sent by the bridegroom to his friends announcing the betrothal and

92

informing them that they would be expected to attend the banquet following the marriage. It is evident that the guests had had ample opportunity to make preparations to be present at the banquet. The custom was such that at the completion of the betrothal period, the bridegroom would proceed to the bride's home to claim her from her father. He would bring her back to his home for the wedding and the subsequent wedding banquet. At this time a second invitation would be sent to the guests, who previously had been invited. This second invitation announced that the time for the banquet had come, that it had been prepared, and that they were expected to present themselves at the banquet. This custom explains why in the parable Christ said, "At the time of the banquet he sent his servant to tell those who had been invited, 'Come, for everything is now ready'" (Luke 14:17). Emphasis seems to be placed on the interval of time between the first and second invitations. These guests had had ample time to prepare to attend the banquet. When Christ referred in the parable to the many guests who had been invited to the banquet, He was speaking symbolically of the nation of Israel. Throughout the Old Testament the promise was given through the prophets that Messiah would come to establish the Davidic kingdom. John the Baptist and Christ offered this kingdom to the nation of Israel (Matt. 3:2; 4:17). During the course of Christ's ministry, the nation had ample opportunity to prepare themselves to respond positively to the invitation and to enter the kingdom that Christ was offering.

But in the parable not all the guests who had been invited heeded the invitation. Instead, "They all alike began to make excuses" (Luke 14:18). In fact, in Christ's day many Israelites did not prepare themselves for the kingdom He offered. The nation as a whole rejected the offer of Himself as Messiah and the kingdom that He had come to institute in fulfillment of the promises and covenants. The parable gives different excuses. Some found their possessions more valuable and of greater concern than the kingdom that Christ offered. Their excuse was "I have just bought a field, and I must go and see it. Please excuse me" (v. 18). They were occupied with their material possessions and did not heed the invitation to follow Christ and enter His kingdom. One sought to be excused due to buying five yoke of oxen and being on the way to try them out. Since one person could work only one yoke of oxen, this one was head of a large business enterprise. This individual was too occupied with business affairs to have time to attend a wedding.

A third person felt that getting married was a justifiable excuse; having recently married, this one read in the law that a man had a year to enjoy his new wife and to become adjusted in the marriage. This one's personal enjoyment stood in the way of entering the kingdom.

In view of the poor response of the invited guests, the host commanded the servant, "Go out quickly into the streets and alleys of the town and bring in the poor, the crippled, the blind and the lame" (Luke 14:21). Such would have been considered defiled and would not have been invited to a banquet. However, Christ was teaching through this parable that in the invitation Messiah was extending, the unacceptable are acceptable to Him if they respond to His invitation. Christ stated by way of the parable that many who fell into this classification responded to the invitation that was extended to them (v. 22). In spite of this response there still was a widespread rejection of the invitation by the nation as a whole, and so there were still seats at the feast. Then, according to the parable, the master commanded his servant again, saying, "Go out to the roads and country lanes and make them come in, so that my house will be full" (v. 23). Those in the byways would represent the Gentiles, who at that time had not had an invitation extended to them to enter the kingdom, since according to Scripture, the kingdom must be established with Israel before Gentiles will enter into millennial blessings (Matt. 10:5-6). But now that Israel had rejected the kingdom offer, an invitation would be extended to Gentiles.

The seriousness of Israel's rejection of the offer given to them is seen in the words "not one of those men who were invited will get a taste of my banquet" (Luke 14:24). Without doubt, those who declined thought only to delay the response and anticipated that there would be ample time for them to enjoy the benefits of the banquet. However, the parable teaches that when Israel rejected the invitation, the offer was withdrawn from them. Thus our Lord answered the question of who will participate in the forthcoming marriage banquet. The invitation did not guarantee participation at the wedding feast, for admission depended on the response. Because of a lack of response, those to whom no invitation was originally extended were later invited and the seats at the wedding feast thus were filled.

THE TOWER BUILDER AND THE KING GOING TO BATTLE
Luke 14:25–33

The works of Christ were so convincing and the words of Christ so winsome that multitudes flocked to Him. Such would readily have called themselves disciples of Jesus. In order to stress the demands made on disciples, Christ taught the attentive crowd what He required of those who would follow Him in truth. First, He said, "If anyone comes to me and does not hate his father and mother, his wife and children, his brothers and sisters—yes, even his own life—he cannot be my disciple" (Luke 14:26). We must understand the Jewish idiom of love and hate. While to us these are manifestations of the emotion, in Scripture these refer to a decision of the will. To love is to choose or to submit to, and to hate is to reject or to refuse to submit. This idiom is clearly illustrated in Malachi 1:2–3, which is quoted in the same sense in Romans 9:13. The prophet declared God's love for Israel, but Israel responded by questioning what demonstration they had had of God's love. The response was "I have loved Jacob; but Esau I have hated" (Mal. 1:2–3). God's love for Jacob was demonstrated in His choice of him to be the heir to the Abrahamic promise, and God showed His hatred of Esau in setting him aside from the line of promise. Thus living and hating were manifestations of God's choice. When Christ demanded that one hate those to whom he is bound by the closest of blood ties, He was not speaking in the area of emotions but in the area of the will. A disciple must make a choice and submit to the authority of Christ rather than to the authority of the family headship.

Christ's next demand was "anyone who does not carry his cross and follow me cannot be my disciple" (Luke 14:27). Christ was not asking that His disciples die physically on a cross as He would die. The cross in the life of Christ was the test of His obedience to the will of God. The cross was to Christ what the tree of the knowledge of good and evil was to Adam in the Garden of Eden. Christ was saying that His disciples must not only choose to follow Him and commit themselves to His headship, but they also must submit themselves to His will. Insisting on one's own will and claiming the right to one's own life exclude one from being a disciple of Christ.

THE PROBLEM

In the light of the rejection of Christ by the religious leaders, life would be perilous for any who committed themselves to Christ and submitted to His will. The leaders would not only reject Christ but reject those who followed Him as well. Those who followed Him might well experience the wrath of the leaders, even as Christ would. This question arose, then: With what attitude should Christ's listeners approach the question of discipleship?

THE SOLUTION

Through parables, Christ instructed those who heeded His words and thus showed themselves to be His disciples. He asserted that they should seriously consider the consequences of such a commitment. First, He related a parable of a man building a tower. The mere desire to build was not a sufficient basis to commence the project. The builder needed to consider the cost involved and see whether sufficient funds were on hand to complete the work. If the tower work were interrupted because of a lack of foresight and preparation, the incompleted building would be a reproach to the builder; and all who noted the lack of planning would offer ridicule. By this parable Christ taught those who were offering themselves to be His disciples to seriously consider the consequences of such a decision. They should see whether they were willing to endure all that would be involved in the total commitment to Him that true discipleship demands.

This consideration was so important that Christ added a second parable. He spoke of a king who was about to engage in battle with an adversary. The mere desire to defeat the adversary was not a sufficient basis on which to proceed. A wise king would number his troops and estimate the size of the enemy force. If he had fewer soldiers than his adversary, he would have to consider whether his soldiers were adequately prepared to take on a numerically superior force. If the careful preparation of his troops and his evaluation of the enemy convinced the king that he was able to gain a victory, then he could proceed into battle. However, if he judged that the adversary was too formidable for his troops, he wisely pursued peace.

In this second parable Christ again pressed on would-be disciples their responsibility to carefully evaluate the strength of the enemy and their own resources. If they were not able to stand against the attack of the one seeking to destroy the kingdom, they should not proceed to the battle. It is not enough to merely want to be a disciple, nor is the attractiveness of being a disciple a sufficient basis for discipleship. One cannot be a true disciple until one first knows what is involved; namely, that one must make a complete commitment to Christ and submit oneself to the will of Christ. Then too one must consider the force of the enemy before making such a commitment. Christ sought disciples who were willing to come to Him on His terms, not on theirs.

THE SEARCHING SHEPHERD, THE SEARCHING WOMAN, AND THE SEEKING FATHER
Luke 15:1-32

THE SETTING

Christ in a previous parable had indicated that He would welcome the outcasts—the poor, the crippled, the blind, and the lame (Luke 14:21). The self-righteous Pharisees quickly took note of those whom Jesus received and welcomed; they observed the kinds of people with whom He enjoyed fellowship and ate meals. The outcasts of society would never have been welcomed by the Pharisees, nor would the Pharisees have considered extending them hospitality at their tables. Such people fell into the classification that the Pharisees called tax collectors and sinners. *Tax collectors* were despised because they had sold themselves to Rome. Under the existing system they became rich at the expense of their fellow Jews as they collected taxes to support Rome. *Sinners* was a broad term that included all the outcasts in society. Christ did not simply tolerate the presence of such people in His company but went further and actually welcomed them and enjoyed fellowship with them. To the Pharisees this meant that Jesus Christ could not possibly be God, for His attitude toward sinners was contrary to what they thought God's attitude toward sinners should be. Their view was that God loved the righteous but hated sinners. They went so far as to say that God delighted in the death of sinners, for this removed sinners from His presence. They had no concept of a God who loved sinners and sought to bring sinners into fellowship with Himself so that He might enjoy fellowship with them. Christ's actions, then, went entirely contrary to the Pharisaic concept of God and gave them a basis on which to reject Christ's claim to be God.

99

THE PROBLEM

The discrepancy between Christ's actions and the Pharisees' concept of God raised the question of what God's attitude was toward sinners. This question was so vital that Christ went into great detail to provide the answer.

THE SOLUTION

While the reply contained three parables, it was collectively a single parable; and Luke referred to Christ's response as "this parable" (Luke 15:3). The following parables are connected to the first by the word "or" (v. 8) and the words "Jesus continued" (v. 11), showing that there are not three replies, but a single reply to the question concerning God's attitude toward sinners.

In introducing the first parable—that of the searching shepherd—Christ did not begin, as was often His custom in parables, by referring to a certain man, which would have made the parable impersonal; instead, He personalized the parable by saying, "Suppose one of you has a hundred sheep and loses one of them" (Luke 15:4). In this way the Lord caused each of His hearers to immediately take personal interest in what was of value to the one who had suffered a loss. Further, Christ's opening statement caused His listeners to evaluate their own responses to such a situation. The Lord knew that because of the value of what had been lost, any of these hearers would have left the ninety-nine to go seek the lost sheep. The search would not have been casual or of short duration; rather, it would have been diligent and would have extended until the valuable lost sheep was found. The search would have been initiated and pursued because of the value placed on what the owner had lost.

When the searcher in the parable had found the lost sheep, he showed his compassion for the animal by putting it on his shoulder and carrying it home. Then at his return he summoned his friends and neighbors to share his joy. The restoration of what was of value to him brought such joy to him that he called others to share in his rejoicing. Christ thus taught that when one is lost,

God the Father searches persistently and diligently for that lost one and finds sufficient joy in the restoration of that lost one to summon others to share His joy. Lest the Pharisees miss the point, Christ explained, "There is more rejoicing in heaven over one sinner who repents than over ninety-nine righteous persons who do not need to repent" (Luke 15:7). Christ was not inferring that the Pharisees, represented by the ninety-nine, were righteous in God's sight. They were righteous in their own sight, and they counted themselves as needing no repentance. The sinner who repented brought joy to God, not the self-righteous Pharisee who rejected Christ's invitation to repentance.

To teach the lesson a second time, Christ used the figure of a woman who had ten silver coins. The coins may have been the bride's dowry that she had been given at her wedding. Such coins were normally mounted on a headband and were worn on the forehead to be publicly seen. The loss of one of the coins would suggest unfaithfulness on the part of the bride to her husband. The coins not only had a monetary value but an emotional value as well, for they signified the bond between the bride and the bridegroom and the faithfulness that such a bond entailed.

In the parable of the lost coin the woman began searching for the coin in her home. Palestinian homes had either a dirt floor or a stone floor. In order to keep down the dust, or to overcome the cold and dampness, the floors would be covered with straw. In order to find a coin that had fallen to the floor, it would be necessary to remove the straw, sift through it, and then sweep the floor. Such a search involved considerable labor, but the coin was of sufficient value that the labor was considered worthwhile. The woman did not shrink from the labor because of the work involved; instead, she searched diligently through the straw until the coin was found. The value of the coin made the labor worthwhile. When she was rewarded for her diligent labor by the discovery of the coin, she experienced such joy that she could not contain it within herself; hence she called her friends and neighbors and invited them to rejoice with her. Once again, Christ, through this parable, revealed that God diligently seeks sinners regardless of the labor involved. When a sinner repents and is restored to God, He rejoices in the sinner's restoration and summons the angels in heaven to join Him in rejoicing over "one sinner who repents" (Luke 15:10).

Christ now proceeded to amplify the lesson by adding a third parable. While emphasis is normally placed on the son, the parable will be misunderstood unless the emphasis is placed on the father, who is mentioned twelve times in the story. Christ was continuing to reveal the attitude of God toward sinners. God's attitude is not reflected by the prodigal son, but rather by the searching father. The son was indeed of a despicable character. He showed his selfishness by asking his father to give him his share of the estate. Such a share would normally have come to him after his father's death, but he asked for the inheritance prematurely so that he might gratify his carnal desires. The father granted his wish. The conduct of the son was like that of Israel, as Psalm 106:14–15 records: "In the desert they gave in to their craving; in the wasteland they put God to the test. So he gave them what they asked for, but sent a wasting disease upon them." Truly the sins of the fathers were practiced by that generation. The son desired to leave the protective oversight of his father and escape responsibility to his father; so he left his father's house and set off for a distant country where he could be totally independent of his father. There he indulged his desires and "squandered his wealth in wild living" (Luke 15:13). Even though his inheritance evidently was large, his indulgences exhausted it. Then the land was paralyzed by a severe famine, which would have quickly escalated the prices of food. The young man had nothing with which to buy even the barest essentials and so he was in dire need. Since he had squandered his entire inheritance, he had to seek employment; and the only job available was that of a swineherd. How utterly degrading for a Jew to be reduced to tending animals whose very presence would bring ceremonial defilement! More adequate provision was made for the pigs than for the swineherd. His wage did not provide sufficient to satisfy his hunger, and so he coveted the very food that he fed the pigs.

But he dared not take food from the pigs to feed himself, and so he was reduced to begging. But because of the famine, no one had food to spare. This son had rejected his father's love and had left his father's home and had repudiated his father's authority, but he could not erase the memory of the abundance that his father had provided for him previously. He began to covet the provision that his father had made for his servants, and he contrasted his present state and the happy condition of his father's servants. This brought to the son the resolution that he would return to his father's home and avail himself of the benefits that his father provided for his servants. The son recognized that there was nothing within him that would commend him to his father. He knew that his father had a just basis for refusing to receive him back into his household if his father wished to punish him. The son, therefore, devised a plan by which he hoped to ingratiate himself sufficiently to his father that his father might bestow on him, not the benefits of a son, but the benefits of a servant. The son recognized the need of confession, and so he proposed to approach his father, saying, "I have sinned against heaven and against you" (Luke 15:18). The son would further acknowledge his unworthiness to be restored to the privileges of sonship that previously had belonged to him by saying, "I am no longer worthy to be called your son" (v. 19). It is to be noted that both of his proposals were true. He had sinned and he was unworthy to be restored. If restoration was granted, it would have to be on some basis other than his worthiness. The son now presented a proposal saying, "Make me like one of your hired men" (v. 19). By faithful service he hoped to ingratiate himself with his father in order to receive benefits from him again. Such were the proposals that the son had in mind when he took the long journey back to his father's house.

Thus far in the parable we have had no revelation of the attitude of God the Father toward sinners, but rather through the son we have had a revelation of the need of sinners. Now, however, the parable proceeds to reveal the Father's attitude toward sinners. The narrative states, "While he was still a long way off, his father saw him" (Luke 15:20). The original Greek puts the emphasis on the words "a long way off," indicating that the father did not remain in his house hoping the son would return. Instead, the father expected the son to return, and so each day the father evidently traveled a considerable distance from the house to a vantage point where he could discern the son's return at the earliest possible moment. Thus this father eagerly anticipated the return of his son.

When the father saw his son, he "was filled with compassion for him" (Luke 15:20). The father's love did not begin with the son's return. The father had never ceased to love his son. He loved his son even when the son was worthy of no love. He loved the son even when the son was estranged from him. He loved the son even when the son was squandering his inheritance in wild living. He loved the son even when the son had stooped to become a swineherd. He loved the son when the son was unworthy of any love. The father's love prompted him to run to his son, to throw his arms around him, and to demonstrate his love by kissing him (v. 20). The son was showered with his father's love that was spontaneously poured out on him. In this parable Christ was emphasizing that God loves sinners and eagerly anticipates their return. The son began to rehearse the carefully prepared plan that he had devised. He acknowledged his sin, saying, "I have sinned against heaven and against you. I am no longer worthy to be called your son" (v. 21). The father did not let the son continue with his offer to become a servant and to work his way back into his father's good graces. Having already demonstrated affection for the son, the father now gave the signal for the son to receive signs signifying his complete restoration to the privileges of sonship. The father commanded the servants, saying, "Bring the best robe and put it on him" (v. 22a). This robe would have the same importance as the robe that Jacob bestowed on Joseph (Gen. 37:3–4), signifying that Joseph had been chosen by his father to be his heir. In Christ's parable, then, the robe signified that this once wayward, but now restored, son was designated as his father's heir. Further, the father commanded the servants to "put a ring on his finger" (v. 22b). The ring was a badge of authority. By impressing the signet ring into wax, business transactions were sealed. The conferring of the ring on the son signified that the father was giving his son the privilege of exercising all the authority that belonged to the father in transacting business in the father's name.

Further, the father commanded the servants, saying, "Put sandals on his feet" (v. 22c). Servants went barefooted. Sandals were a sign that the son was not a servant. This one who came to offer himself as a servant was to receive sandals that would set him apart from the servants in the father's household.

In addition, the father expressed his joy at his son's return by commanding the servants to "bring the fattened calf and kill it. Let's have a feast and celebrate" (Luke 15:23). The fact that a calf had already been fattened indicates that the father had been anticipating the son's return. The calf that had been prepared in view of the anticipated return of the son was now to be sacrificed. Just as the shepherd found joy in finding the lost sheep (v. 6) and the woman found joy in finding the lost coin (v. 9), so the father found joy in the return and the restoration of his son. This joy was such that it must be shared. Thus the parable teaches that God loves sinners, that God searches for sinners, that God restores sinners, and that God confers the privileges and blessings of sonship on those who return to Him. On the one hand, these three parables adequately refuted the error of the Pharisees who insisted that God hates sinners and rejoices in their death. On the other hand, these parables reveal God's love for sinners and the blessings that God confers on those who return to Him.

Christ continued the parable by introducing the older son. He did so in order to further expose the attitude of the Pharisees toward sinners and their attitude toward God when He receives sinners. While the younger son's return was being celebrated at the banquet, the older son was in the field. He was not invited to share in the banquet, for the father knew that the older son would find no joy in the younger son's return and restoration. As the older son came near the house, he heard the sounds of rejoicing and he asked one of the servants attending the banquet what was going on. He was informed that his younger brother had returned, that their father had killed the calf that had been prepared for the son's return, and that the father was rejoicing at the son's return.

The attitude of the older son toward his father was that he "became angry and refused to go in" (Luke 15:28). He did not rejoice that his younger brother had returned and had been restored. In this part of the parable Christ was revealing that when the Pharisees criticized Him for welcoming sinners and eating with them, they were, in fact, criticizing the God who loves sinners and welcomes them on their return. That this son could have partaken in the banquet is evident from the fact that "his father went out and pleaded with him" (v. 28). The father's plea was a plea to the son to change his attitude toward his father and toward his brother who had returned, for he could not expect this son to attend the banquet until the son changed his attitude. However, the son refused to change his attitude or participate in the celebration. He charged his father with injustice, saying, "All these years I've been slaving for you and never disobeyed your orders. Yet you never gave me even a young goat so I could celebrate with my friends" (v. 29). The older son was saying that his father had withheld from him the reward for his service that was rightly his. The older son was contrasting the treatment that the younger son had received and his own treatment by the father. The older son thought his father had acted unjustly for withholding such benefits from him. To this the father replied, "You are always with me, and everything I have is yours" (v. 31). By this Christ was revealing that the same privileges that were afforded the younger son were always available to the older son. But the older son had never availed himself of what the father would have bestowed on him. Therefore the older son could not blame the father for the fact that he did not have what the younger son was now enjoying. The father had provided these blessings for the older son, who had never availed himself of what the father had made available. The fault, then, was not with the father, but with the older son. In this part of the parable, Christ was seeking to convey to the Pharisees that even though they called themselves the servants of God and the sons of God, they were revealing by their attitude toward God that they were not true servants and they were not considered sons. God had made available to them the same privileges that He made available to the sinner who returned to Him. However, the Pharisees had not come to God in order to receive from Him the benefits that He had provided; in spite of their profession of sonship, they were not considered sons. If they would do as the younger son did—that is, come to God and acknowledge their sinfulness and unworthiness—they could receive from Him the same blessings and privileges conferred on the sinner who repented.

Thus in these three parables Christ made it very clear why He welcomed sinners and ate with them. He demonstrated the compassion of God for sinners. Contrary to the thinking of the Pharisees, God receives sinners instead of rejecting them. Contrary to the doctrine of the Pharisees, God does not rejoice in the death of sinners, but rather He rejoices when sinners are restored to fellowship with Himself. God delights to bestow on the unworthy the privileges of sonship, and such privileges would be extended even to the Pharisees if they would do what the wayward son did—return to the Father, acknowledge their sinfulness, accept His forgiveness, and then enter into the privileges of sonship.

THE FORESIGHTED MANAGER
Luke 16:1–13

THE SETTING

At this time in His ministry, Christ was dealing with many of the erroneous attitudes of the Pharisees. He had dealt with their hypocrisies (Luke 12:1), their coveteousness (v. 15), their love of preeminence (14:11), their concept of God (15:2), and their refusal to repent (v. 29). He now preceeded to give a series of parables to correct their erroneous attitude toward money. The purpose, however, was not only to rebuke the Pharisees but to instruct the disciples in these important matters.

THE PROBLEM

The Pharisees were characterized as lovers of money (Luke 16:14). To them the acquisition of wealth was the highest good in life. In Deuteronomy 28 God had promised material blessings to those who obeyed the law. The Pharisees concluded that all wealth was necessarily a sign of divine approval. They, therefore, devoted themselves to acquiring what they considered to be the sign of their acceptance by God. They made ostentatious displays of such wealth in an effort to convince people that they were righteous. However, such an interpretation of wealth was false and such a use of wealth was wrong. Since the Pharisaic example was incorrect, the question arose, How, then, should wealth be used?

THE SOLUTION

It was customary for a wealthy man to entrust the oversight of his goods to a trusted manager and thus relieve himself of the daily administration of household affairs. The wealth of this rich man was in olive oil and wheat. The man evidently owned much land, and so he could produce a large harvest. He entrusted his wealth to his manager to the extent that he made no effort to check on that one's administration of the goods. After an ex-

tended period of time, a report concerning his manager's mis-
management of the goods came to the owner's attention. It seems
evident that the manager's wrong oversight was well known in the
community long before the owner learned of it. This misman-
agement led to the manager's dismissal. It thus became necessary
for the manager to tally the goods that remained in order to report
to the owner what was now on hand.

Up to this point, the future of the manager had been secure;
but now through the loss of his appointment, his future was
insecure. There were few options that readily presented themselves to the manager. The first was to take a menial laborer's job.
But he eliminated this as a possibility because he was physically
unable to perform such rigorous work. The second alternative
was to beg. This was too humiliating for the manager to even
consider in the light of the past privileges he had enjoyed and the
honor that his position had brought to him. The manager then
thought of a third alternative. He still had a brief time before his
appointment was terminated. He could exercise his authority as
administrator in this final period to gain friends so that when he
lost his job these newly found friends would provide for him. In
order to accomplish this the manager called in those who were
heavily indebted to his master. The first owed eight hundred
gallons of olive oil. The manager had this debtor rewrite the bill,
cutting the indebtedness in half. The second owed one thousand
bushels of wheat. The manager sought to ingratiate himself to
this debtor by having the person rewrite the bill, making it now
eight hundred bushels. However, in doing so, the manager was
acting dishonestly (Luke 16:8), for he was responsible for his
master's goods. In reducing the indebtedness, the manager was
cheating his master out of what was rightly his. Instead of concerning himself with the good of his master, the manager was
acting selfishly and was considering only his own good. Thus he
was dishonest.

However, when what he had done came to the attention of the
owner, the latter commended "the dishonest manager because he
had acted shrewdly" (Luke 16:8). The owner did not commend

the manager for his dishonesty or for his selfishness but for his shrewdness. The manager used his present opportunities with a view to receiving future rewards. In that sense he acted wisely. A foolish person lives only for the present and uses personal wealth only for the present. A wise person considers the future and uses personal wealth to reap benefits in the future; the person of the world accepts this use of wealth as a fundamental business principle. Christ observed that "the people of this world are more shrewd in dealing with their own kind than are the people of the light" (v. 8). Christ was saying that His disciples should use sound business principles and use their time, privilege, and wealth, not for the present, but with a view to future remuneration.

Christ applied this principle by exhorting His disciples to be faithful in the use of what has been entrusted to them, saying, "Whoever can be trusted with very little can also be trusted with much. . . . So if you have not been trustworthy in handling worldly wealth, who will trust you with true riches?" (Luke 16:10–11). Christ concluded His instruction to His disciples concerning wealth in this parable by reminding, "No servant can serve two masters. Either he will hate the one and love the other, or he will be devoted to the one and despise the other. You cannot serve both God and Money" (v. 13). Christ was using love and hate according to Jewish idiom. These are manifestations of the will, not of the emotions. The one who loves chooses and submits to what is the object of the affection. The one who hates turns from and refuses to submit to what is the object of hatred. Christ made it very clear that one cannot serve God and be the servant of money at the same time. It is impossible for one to serve two masters simultaneously, for the two masters will never agree on what they expect from the one who serves them. The disciple, then, must make a choice as to whether to name Christ as Master, or whether money will be master.

THE RICH MAN AND THE BEGGAR
Luke 16:19–31

THE SETTING

The Pharisees' love of money was so deep-rooted in both their theology and their practice that Christ spoke a second parable in this context in order to correct the misunderstanding of His disciples and to instruct them in the proper evaluation of money.

THE PROBLEM

Out of our Lord's previous parable the following questions quite naturally would arise: What is the danger of serving money? What is the result of giving oneself to the pursuit of material possessions?

THE SOLUTION

The beginning of the parable is a study in contrasts between a rich man and a poor man. The rich man was able to indulge himself with all of the luxuries of life. He made ostentatious displays of his accumulated wealth as he paraded in purple and fine linen before people. In contrast was a beggar who was too weak to walk because of his hunger and disease. This beggar was laid at the gate of the wealthy man. He was there seeking alms and hoping that his misery would generate mercy in the rich man, who could meet his need. Influenced by Pharisaic theology, the wealthy man would have considered himself righteous before God because of the wealth that he had accumulated. However, the fact that he showed no mercy demonstrated that he was not righteous, for the law said one evidence of righteousness is that one loves one's neighbor as oneself (Luke 10:27). Although the wealthy man saw the need of the beggar who was laid at his gate and was able to meet the need, he made no response to the beggar's need. Thus the rich man demonstrated that he had not fulfilled the righteousness that the law demanded and therefore was not righteous in the sight of God. It was not necessary for the rich man to seek out his "neighbor" in order to show mercy, for his "neighbor" had been laid at his gate. The rich man had had many opportunities to show mercy but had consistently refused to do so. Christ now proceeded in the parable to show the respective destinies of the two men. As great as was their contrast in life, even greater was their contrast in death. "The beggar died and the angels carried him to Abraham's side" (Luke 16:22). "Abraham's side" was a Jewish idiom for the presence of God. According to Pharisaic theology, the beggar was poor because he was wicked; and he was hated by God. The Pharisees thought God would cast such a one from His presence at death. However, Jesus taught that the beggar was taken into God's presence. After the rich man died, according to Pharisaic doctrine, he should have been transported immediately to God's presence and welcomed to the joys of eternal life. However, Jesus taught that the rich man was excluded from the presence of God and was cast into hades. Instead of enjoying blessing, he was tormented. The one who had despised the beggar and prided himself that he was not like the beggar now envied the beggar, for he could see the joys into which the beggar had been brought. Jesus taught in this part of the parable that wealth is not necessarily a sign of God's approval, nor is the possession of wealth a guarantee of entrance into eternal life. The rich man trusted his riches to redeem him, and he had his part in hell. The beggar was "poor in spirit" (Matt. 5:3) as well as poor in material blessings; because he was poor in spirit, he had his part in the presence of God. Christ frequently likened the torment of eternal punishment to the burning of fire. The rich man experienced this torment and begged that God would now show mercy to him by sending the beggar "to dip the tip of his finger in water and cool my tongue" (Luke 16:24). It is ironic that the rich man, who refused to show any mercy to Lazarus in his need, now begged that Lazarus might be the instrument to show mercy to him in his need. The rich man confessed the greatness of his torment, saying, "I am in agony in this fire" (v. 24). Thus far Christ has revealed that the possession of riches does not guarantee salvation, nor does the absence of riches preclude salvation. Since Christ has shown that money cannot save, He has exposed the danger of enslaving oneself to money. One who trusts in money is entrusting one's eternal destiny to what cannot save.

In the parable Christ now proceeded to show that material things have only temporary, not eternal, value. Abraham responded to the petition of the rich man for relief by addressing him as "Son" (Luke 16:25). He was Abraham's son, or descendant, in the flesh, but he was not related to Abraham through faith; and without Abraham's faith, the rich man could not be saved. According to rabbinical teaching, the Pharisees believed that Father Abraham sat at the gate of hades and would not let one of his sons pass through. The wealthy man felt that he was eternally safe because he was wealthy and was a physical descendant of Abraham. Christ was showing that neither reason was sufficient for salvation. The material wealth that the rich man possessed could be enjoyed only during his lifetime on earth. His earthly wealth could not be transferred to the heavenly realm even though, as Christ had taught in a previous parable, such wealth could be used during one's lifetime to obtain eternal reward (cf. Luke 12:17–21). Were the possessions transferable, the wealthy man could have used them to pipe water from a cool spring to satisfy his burning thirst!

Christ indicated very clearly that at death one's eternal destiny is settled. Between those in the presence of God and those in hades "a great chasm has been fixed, so that those who want to go from here to you cannot, nor can anyone cross over from there to us" (Luke 16:26). While the merciful who are in the presence of God might be moved by the misery of those who are separated from God, it is impossible for them to minister to the needs of the miserable. Their destiny was settled at physical death.

The memory of the rich man's past was not erased from his mind. He could remember! He could recall his false confidence in wealth and his wrong devotion to it. He could recall the opportunity that he had to use his wealth in showing mercy and thus to demonstrate that he was righteous. And he knew that his brothers even now had the same attitude that had characterized him and that had brought him to his present state; and he expressed his concern for them. He begged that Lazarus might be sent to his brothers to warn them of the peril of trusting wealth to obtain salvation. He concluded that they would be moved by the reappearance of one who had been restored from the dead. But Abraham replied, "They have Moses and the Prophets; let them listen to them" (v. 29). The Law and the Prophets bore testimony to God's requirement for fellowship with Himself and revealed the way by which people can be accepted by God. The testimony of the Law and the Prophets was sufficient, and no added witness was necessary to bring people to faith.

Thus Christ answered the pressing question of why it was dangerous to trust in riches by showing that riches cannot provide salvation and that riches are only temporary. Further, Christ showed that one's eternal destiny is settled at death and that a person's previous wealth is of no use to the one who has entered the eternal state. If wealth is used selfishly, it will perish; but if it is used as a means of showing mercy it can gain eternal reward.

THE UNWORTHY SLAVE
Luke 17:7–10

THE SETTING

Christ through parables has been giving instruction to the disciples as to their responsibility to Him. In Luke 17 the Lord warned them against following a course of conduct that would be a bad example and thus could lead other people to sin. He had also instructed the disciples about their obligation to forgive one who has sinned against them. They recognized that they needed faith to accept Christ's instructions and the consequent obligations imposed by His teachings. Christ's instructions were so overwhelming that the apostles cried, "Increase our faith!" (Luke 17:5). Christ's reply was "If you have faith as small as a mustard seed, you can say to this mulberry tree, 'Be uprooted and planted in the sea,' and it will obey you" (v. 6). Christ was saying that they did not need increased faith; rather, they needed to exercise the faith that they already possessed in order to discharge the obligations placed on them by the knowledge He had conveyed.

THE PROBLEM

This parable answers two questions: "What is the obligation of a disciple to Christ? What attitude should a disciple have while serving Christ?"

THE SOLUTION

In this parable Christ was not referring to a hired servant who had committed himself for a day's labor at an agreed wage. Instead, the parable revolves around a slave who was the purchased possession of the master. Christ was viewing the apostles, not as hired servants, but as bond slaves who belonged to Him by virtue of purchase. The servant in the parable had spent the day plowing in a field or tending sheep. He would have done this in accordance with his master's will. Christ was emphasizing that the

115

slaveholder has the right to command slaves and that the responsibility of slaves is to discharge the work the owner has given them to do. They would have worked from sunup to sundown to discharge the responsibilities assigned to them. As evening fell the slaves returned exhausted and hungry from the day's labor. In the parable the slave was not released from obligation to further service because of what he had already completed. Rather, he was commanded, "Prepare my supper, get yourself ready and wait on me while I eat and drink; after that you may eat and drink" (Luke 17:8). The slaveholder had a right to expect further service from slaves. The needs of the owner took precedence over the needs of slaves. Therefore, their personal needs were subjected to the demands of the slaveholder.

Christ then raised the question, "Would he thank the servant because he did what he was told to do?" (v. 9), and the answer was no. The slaveholder had been exercising his right, and the slave had fulfilled his responsibility as the purchased possession of. the owner. Thanks was not due them because this was their rightful obligation. Christ then applied the parable to the apostles, saying, "So you also, when you have done everything you were told to do, should say, 'We are unworthy servants; we have only done our duty'" (v. 10). In this parable Christ viewed the disciples as His purchased possessions and Himself as their Lord. He saw them as obligated to discharge His will as He revealed it to them. Such was their indebtedness to Him because of His purchase of them. Christ set no limits as to what He might ask of them, nor no bounds on their obligation to Him. Their obligation to Him would be reiterated in the upper room when He addressed the Eleven and said, "I no longer call you servants, because a servant does not know his master's business. Instead, I have called you friends, for everything that I learned from my Father I have made known to you. You did not choose me, but I chose you to go and bear fruit—fruit that will last" (John 15:15–16). Here their obligation was not that of slavery but that of love. But love placed an even greater responsibility on them that their relationship to Christ as slaves had produced.

THE PERSISTENT WIDOW
Luke 18:1–8

THE SETTING

In response to the disciple's request that the Lord teach them to pray (Luke 11:1), He had told them to keep on asking, seeking, and knocking. As noted earlier Luke 11:10 can be translated, "For everyone who keeps on asking receives; he who keeps on seeking finds; and to him who keeps on knocking, the door will be opened." Lest this important truth should be lost to the disciples, Christ told a parable to stress the importance of persistence in prayer.

THE PROBLEM

Having heard our Lord's instruction, the disciples might well have faced the following question: What benefits come from persistence in prayer?

THE SOLUTION

In order to answer the question, Christ introduced the figure of a judge. His responsibility was to serve as an arbiter and to administer justice. One who had been wronged by another would present the case to the judge, who then saw that justice was served. Jesus specifically called attention to the character of this administrator of justice. The judge "neither feared God nor cared about men" (Luke 18:2). Such a one would not be expected to respond to an appeal based either on righteousness or on emotion. Nevertheless, he bore the responsibility to administer justice. A widow came to this judge to present her plea. She had been wronged and, because she was a widow, she had no one to present her cause. Therefore, she presented her own cause to the judge in an effort to obtain justice.

Because of his insensitivity, the judge at first refused to rectify the wrong that had been done to this widow. However, the widow's cause was just, and so she persisted in asking the judge for justice. His indifference and lack of sense of responsibility in

117

the discharge of his office did not dissuade the widow. She presented her cause again and again. Her sense of the rightness of her cause made her persistent in her petition.

Because of her persistence, the judge eventually was moved to rectify the wrong; and he determined to see that she got justice. However, even though he aided the woman, the judge was still of a selfish character and did not care about justice. He simply wanted to relieve himself of the bother that the woman's persistence brought to him.

The Lord was showing the disciples that one who has a right cause may rightly persist in pursuing it. Even an unjust, uncaring judge may be brought to dispense justice by persistence. Christ now drew a contrast, saying, "Will not God bring about justice for his chosen ones, who cry out to him day and night? Will he keep putting them off? I tell you, he will see that they get justice, and quickly" (Luke 18:7–8). If an unjust judge can be brought to administer judgment in response to the persistent plea of one who presents a right cause, will not a just and merciful God respond to those who present a persistent plea to Him for what is right?

In His initial instruction on prayer, Christ had commanded the disciples to pray, "Your kingdom come, your will be done on earth as it is in heaven" (Matt. 6:10). The kingdom that Christ offered was being rejected and the King was being repudiated. Christ counseled His disciples to persist in prayer, despite the opposition, with the assurance that God would hear and would answer prayer. God would respond to their petition and grant their request in the kingdom. Although postponed, the kingdom would one day be established; those who opposed the kingdom would be judged and the righteous who anticipated the kingdom would be vindicated. Christ closed the parable with a question: "When the Son of Man comes, will he find faith on the earth?" (v. 8). The context shows that Christ anticipated a negative answer. The Lord was saying that the disciples were to persist in faith in spite of continued opposition and rejection and that God in His own time would grant their request "Your kingdom come."

THE PHARISEE AND THE TAX COLLECTOR
Luke 18:9–14

In the broad context Christ had been giving instructions to the disciples concerning prayer. In the parable of the persistent widow, He had shown that one with a proper petition should persist in prayer until that for which one has been praying has been received.

THE PROBLEM

Two questions would arise in the minds of those whom the Lord was instructing concerning prayer: What is the basis of prayer? What is the ground of one's approach to God? The Pharisees felt they were capable of approaching God on the basis of their own righteousness. There were others who felt that they needed a righteousness other than their own in order to be heard by God. These questions, then, demanded answers because of the theological controversy over this issue.

THE SOLUTION

This parable was not addressed primarily to the disciples, but rather to those "who were confident of their own righteousness and looked down on everybody else" (Luke 18:9). Thus we see that the Pharisees were in view and that Christ was seeking to correct their false doctrine. In the parable "two men went up to the temple to pray" (v. 10). The people believed that prayer would more readily be heard if addressed to God in the temple area. The Old Testament records that God dwelt in the tabernacle for a time; later God chose the temple as His dwelling place. It was in the Holy of Holies in these places of worship that the shekinah glory of God dwelt, and from these most holy places God revealed His Presence to the people. The people were compelled to assemble periodically at the tabernacle or the temple in order to observe the appointed feasts. These places, then, became the appointed places of worship. Thus in order to fulfill their obligation to offer prayer to God, the two men went up to the temple. One of these men, a Pharisee, was confident that his own righteousness would commend him to God. The other, a tax collector, was despised by the people.

The Pharisee by his very posture demonstrated his self-righteous arrogance, for in praying he stood erect. In praying he did not concern himself with the attributes of God, but rather with the righteousnesses that he thought he possessed. He set himself apart from "all other men" whom he classified as "robbers, evildoers, adulterers—or . . . tax collector[s]" (Luke 18:11).

The Pharisees as a religious sect considered only themselves to be righteous and characterized all who were not part of their party as sinners and thus unacceptable to God. The Pharisee in the parable was typical; he recited the outward evidences of his professed righteousness. He fasted twice a week and gave a tenth of his income. In fasting and tithing he considered himself to have fulfilled the righteousness of the law. He seems to have been entirely oblivious that Christ in the Sermon on the Mount (Matt. 5–7) had taught that God does not count external observances of tradition as righteousnesses; rather, what God requires and accepts is an internal righteousness that is evidenced by external acts. The Pharisee not only was commending himself to God, but he was seeking to demonstrate to those passing through the temple area how pious and upright he was. The prayer, then, was not to honor God but to bring honor to himself from those who would observe him in his public praying.

The tax collector approached the place of prayer in quite a different attitude. First, he "stood at a distance" (Luke 18:13a). He recognized that he was a sinner and unworthy to come into the presence of God. He dared not even approach the temple where God was thought to be dwelling. Further, "he would not even look up to heaven" (v. 13b). This, again, was an outward

sign of his recognition of his own unworthiness. He dropped his
eyes and stared toward the ground instead of looking toward the
place where God was thought to dwell. Again, he "beat his
breast" (v. 13c). The beating of the breast was a sign of mourning,
of remorse, and of contrition. He not only recognized that he was
a sinner, but he was acknowledging his sin and was giving an
outward sign of repentance because of his sin. He then voiced his
petition, saying, "God, have mercy on me, a sinner" (v. 13d).
When we properly understand this petition, we discover the answer to the question, What is the basis for acceptable prayer? The
man was not asking for clemency. He was not asking God to
overlook the sin. He was not asking God to change His attitude
toward him. Rather, the man was putting himself under blood
and pleading blood as the basis on which he might approach
God, even though he recognized that he was a sinner. His petition, quite literally, reads in the Greek, "God, be propitiated to
me, a sinner" (cf. v. 13d).

The petitioner evidently had in mind the ritual of the Day of
Atonement, which was the foundation of the relationship of the
nation of Israel to God. At the time of the Exodus, God redeemed His covenant people from their bondage to Egypt so that
they came to be referred to as a redeemed people. Isaiah so
referred to them, saying, "Fear not, for I have redeemed you; I
have called you by name; you are mine" (Isa. 43:1). The reference of the prophet was to the redemption of the nation out of
Egypt. At the Exodus the nation had become a people for God's
own possession by purchase, with blood being the purchase price.
That nation, however, did not walk as a redeemed people should;
instead, they strayed from the path of obedience. When God
brought the nation to Sinai, He revealed to them the basis on
which He would maintain a relationship with them. At Sinai,
God established the ritual of the Day of Atonement (Lev. 16).
The details of the ritual of that significant day were to be performed by God's appointed priests. Special garments were provided for the high priest and were to be worn only on this occasion. Before donning the garments the priest had to bathe (Lev.

16:4), for one who is unclean could not perform the rituals of this significant day. Following his cleansing and robing, the high priest was to select two male goats for a sin offering and a ram for a burnt offering (v. 5). The high priest first offered a bull to make atonement for himself (v. 6). His sins had to be covered by blood before he could represent the nation in making an offering to cover their sins. After he was thus covered by blood, he was to slaughter the goat of the sin offering on behalf of the people. He took the blood in a basin and sprinkled it on the atonement cover, that is, the cover of the ark of the Testimony (Lev. 16:15; cf. Exod. 25:17). In the ark had been placed the stone tablets of the covenant that God had given to Moses, a gold jar of manna, and Aaron's rod that had budded (Heb. 9:4). Atonement was necessary because the nation had violated the law that God had given to guide their conduct. Having broken the law, they were sinners in the sight of God; and God could not dwell in the midst of a sinful people. When blood was applied to the atonement cover, blood was interposed between the God whose glory was revealed above the atonement cover and who dwelt between the two cherubim and the law that was contained in the ark beneath the atonement cover. This application of the blood to cover the broken law was a propitiatory act. The blood propitiated, and God was the One who was propitiated. The people who had violated the law were those for whom propitiation was made. The atonement cover was the place of propitiation. By this propitiatory act, God was provided with a basis for dwelling among a people whose sins had been covered by blood. After offering this propitiatory covering, the high priest emerged from the Holy of Holies and took the second goat (Lev. 16:20). He confessed over this goat the sins of the people and committed that goat into the hands of a trustworthy person, who then led the goat away into the desert (vv. 21–22). This signified the removal of the nation's sins that had been put under that propitiatory covering. God could continue to dwell among the people and own them as His own because He had been propitiated. He was satisfied with the atoning sacrifice and so was provided a basis by which He could dwell among this sinful people. God would continue among the people for another twelve months, after which the ritual must be repeated. The ritual had to be annually observed because, as the writer to the Hebrews tells us, "It is impossible for the blood of bulls and goats to take away sins" (Heb. 10:4).

The offering on the Day of Atonement was national; it was for Israel as a nation. In contrast, if an individual sinned, he was restored to fellowship with the God against whom he had sinned by offering one of the sin offerings of Leviticus 4–5. The offerings of Leviticus 1–3 were expressions of worship and thanksgiving and these offerings were "an aroma pleasing to the LORD" (1:9; 2:2; 3:5). The offerings of Leviticus 1–5 could benefit the individual only because of the national offering on the Day of Atonement. Without that national offering, the individual offerings would have been pointless. According to the law, the offerings were to be offered only for unintentional sins. In the case of a willful sin, one did not offer the prescribed individual sin offering; rather, one put oneself under the blood of the Day of Atonement. David did this after his sin with Bathsheba. Knowing he had committed a willful sin and that there was no prescribed offering, he fled to the atonement cover, crying, "Have mercy on me, O God, according to your unfailing love; according to your great compassion blot out my transgressions. Wash away all my iniquity and cleanse me from my sin. For I know my transgressions, and my sin is always before me. Against you, you only, have I sinned and done what is evil in your sight. . . . Cleanse me with hysop, and I will be clean; wash me, and I will be whiter than snow" (Ps. 51:1–4, 7). In putting himself under the blood of the atonement cover, David once again experienced the joy of his salvation (v. 12).

When the tax collector in the parable prayed, "Have mercy on me, a sinner" (Luke 18:13), he was doing what David did. He was asking God to look on him as he looked on the atonement cover. Because the man took refuge under the propitiating blood, Christ declared, "This man, rather than the other, went home justified before God" (v. 14). Prayer is not based on a person's own righteousness, but rather it is possible because a sinner has found forgiveness by putting himself under the propitiating blood.

The ritual of the Day of Atonement was designed to foreshadow the work of Jesus Christ on the cross, where a propitiatory sacrifice was offered. God was the One propitiated, for the offering was made to Him (Heb. 9:14). The body of Christ was the place of propitiation (1 Peter 2:24). The blood of Christ was that which propitiated (Heb. 9:22–28). The propitiation of the Cross was for all sinners whether past, present, or future. Its benefits come to all who look to God in faith (1 John 2:2). Thus we would learn from the parable that sinful people cannot approach God on the basis of their own righteousness, but only through the benefit of the blood of Christ that was shed as a propitiatory act to provide God a basis for hearing and accepting sinners. Therefore, prayer is to be offered in Jesus' name.

THE LABORERS IN THE VINEYARD
Matthew 20:1–16

THE SETTING

In the preceding context Christ had been approached by someone who asked, "Teacher, what good thing must I do to get eternal life?" (Matt. 19:16). This man possessed great wealth (v. 22). Luke mentioned that he was a "ruler" (Luke 18:18). This meant that he was a scholar in the law and that his knowledge of the law had elevated him to a position of authority on the Sanhedrin, even though he was still considered a young man (Matt. 19:20). Because of his position, knowledge, and wealth, such a one would have been considered by Pharisaic standards to be acceptable to God and already in the kingdom. The question asked by this ruler was like the question asked by an expert in the law in Luke 10:25. The ruler was concerned with matters of righteousness, and he was seeking Christ's interpretation as to how righteous one must be to enter the kingdom that He had offered. Christ asked the man why he addressed this question to Him, since God alone is good or righteous and has the right to determine the standards of righteousness that are required for entrance into His kingdom. In this indirect way Christ was causing the man to face the question concerning His person. If He was God, as He claimed to be, then His answer would be authoritative. In order to define the goodness that God expects, Christ directed the man to the commandments. He was not inferring that the man would obtain righteousness by keeping the commandments, but rather that the commandments revealed the standard of righteousness that God requires for entrance into His kingdom. According to Pharisaic tradition, there were some 248 commandments and 365 prohibitions. When Christ told him to obey the commandments, the man was overwhelmed at the enormity of the requirement and sought to reduce the obligation by inquiring, "Which ones?" (Matt. 19:18). Christ then sum-

125

marized the second table of the law, which governs the responsibility that people have to other people. The young man replied
that he had kept all of these (v. 20). Again following Pharisaic
tradition, he deemed that because he had not committed certain
external acts, he had not violated the law. Instead of identifying
individual acts that would have proved the young man a violator,
as He well might have done, Christ put the man to the test by
telling him to sell all of his possessions, distribute the proceeds to
the poor, and then come and follow Him as a disciple. The
young man could not pass this test, for he loved his material
possessions too much. In departing from Christ, the young man
showed that he had not fulfilled the first commandment of the
law, which was to love God above all else (v. 22). That the young
man was trusting his riches for salvation was evident, for Christ
said to the disciples, "It is hard for a rich man to enter the
kingdom of heaven" (v. 23). A man who has riches may enter the
kingdom, but a man who trusts his riches will never enter the
kingdom. Christ was not stressing the difficulty of a man who
trusts in his riches to enter the kingdom; instead, He was teaching
the impossibility of entering. We see this from the fact that Christ
referred to a literal camel and physician's suturing needle. Christ
said that as a camel cannot go through the eye of the needle, one
who trusts his riches cannot enter the kingdom. The response of
the disciples showed that they were still thinking traditionally.
They asked, "Who then can be saved?" (v. 25). They meant, If
one on whom God has bestowed wealth as a sign of His approval
cannot be saved, how could a poor man ever be saved? Christ's
reply was that salvation is of God: "With man this is impossible,
but with God all things are possible" (v. 26).

THE PROBLEM

Having heard the discussion with the young man, Peter addressed a question to Christ: "We have left everything to follow
you! What then will there be for us?" (Matt. 19:27). In response
to Christ's call, Peter had left his gainful employment as a
fisherman; he had forsaken his business, his income, his home,

his family, and all else to follow Christ. He therefore was curious concerning the rewards that he could expect.

THE SOLUTION

In response to Peter's request, Christ made the great promise concerning the kingdom He had offered to Israel but which had been postponed. Christ said that when the kingdom is eventually instituted, "you who have followed me will also sit on twelve thrones, judging the twelve tribes of Israel" (Matt. 19:28). Positions of honor in the coming kingdom would be conferred on the ones who had followed Him. Then, in the parable that follows, Christ revealed the basis on which rewards will be distributed to those who have left all to commit themselves to Him. Christ told of a landowner who went to the marketplace early in the morning to hire laborers for his vineyard. While some land was worked by slaves, other land was worked by hired men. It was customary for those who desired employment to assemble in the marketplace at daybreak. One desiring to hire employees for the day would go to the marketplace, select laborers, and agree on the wage for the day's work. The laborers thus hired would go to the fields and work until sunset, at which time they would receive their wages and return home. The process was repeated daily. On the occasion to which the Lord referred, the landowner had hired a retinue of men and agreed to pay a denarius, which was the accepted daily wage.

The landowner returned to the marketplace in the third, sixth, ninth, and eleventh hours. Each time he returned he found that additional workers had come to the marketplace seeking employment. Since there was more work to be done than could be accomplished by those hired early in the morning, the landowner put them to work with the stipulation that he would pay them what was right. Since the added laborers had joined the work at later periods in the day, they could not reasonably expect to receive the same wage that he had stipulated for those who began their labor at sunup. At the close of the working day, the workers came to receive their wages. Those who had worked only an hour received a denarius. In this the landowner was showing his generosity toward the laborers, for those who had worked such a short time had no basis to expect to be remunerated so generously. Having observed the graciousness of the owner in paying these workers, other workers who had labored through the day assumed that they also would receive much more than their stipulated wage. However, the landowner gave them what he had promised—a denarius. By complaining, these revealed that they did not understand the graciousness of their employer. "They began to grumble against the landowner" (v. 11), voicing their objections. The landowner's reply to a worker called attention to his justice in paying wages, for he reminded him that he had given him what he had agreed to pay. The landowner had certainly not robbed these workers of what was rightly theirs. But then the landowner stressed graciousness as well as justice when he asked, "Don't I have the right to do what I want with my own money?" (v. 15). Thus the fault was not in him but in them.

By this parable Christ was answering Peter's question "What then will there be for us?" (Matt. 19:27). Christ was saying that disciples are to fulfill the work entrusted to them, leaving the distribution of the reward to Him. The Lord is just, gracious, and generous; and He will do what is right. The parable encourages us who have been called to serve Christ at the end of the age to be faithful, for we may graciously receive a reward equal to that received by those who were first called to Christ as His laborers and who endured so much suffering and even death for His name's sake.

THE TEN MINAS
Luke 19:11-27

THE SETTING

In the context preceding the parable of the ten minas, we have a record of the conversion of Zacchaeus of Jericho, who was "a chief tax collector and was wealthy" (Luke 19:2). Zacchaeus had entered into contract with the Roman government to collect taxes in his area, and he had gathered a number of tax collectors who worked under him. He was a man of great influence in the Roman system and by his position had gained great wealth. But he was held in utter contempt by the Jews, who saw him as an instrument of the despised Roman government and counted him among the lowest of sinners.

The reputation of Christ had preceded Him; and so when He came to Jericho, Zacchaeus sought Him out. It was necessary for Zacchaeus to climb into the lower branches of a sycamore-fig tree to see over the crowd. Christ knew the reason that Zacchaeus desired to see Him, and He summoned him down from his observation point. The Lord then requested hospitality from him, which Zacchaeus most gladly extended. After they had entered the home of Zacchaeus, he said, "Here and now I give half of my possessions to the poor, and if I have cheated anybody out of anything, I will pay back four times the amount" (Luke 19:8). In doing this Zacchaeus demonstrated the fruits of repentance. Such fruits could only stem from faith in the person of Christ. Zacchaeus was showing that he had met the demands for entrance into the kingdom, spoken first by John the Baptist and then later by Christ. Christ accepted these works of Zacchaeus as a validation of his faith and declared, "Today salvation has come to this house, because this man, too, is a son of Abraham" (v. 9). God had made a covenant with Abraham that promised blessings to the patriarch's physical descendants. Since Zacchaeus was a physical descendant of Abraham, he was eligible to receive the

129

blessings that would come to Abraham's descendants who exercised Abraham's faith. Christ's explanation of why He would willingly receive one held in such ill repute was "the Son of Man came to seek and to save what was lost" (v. 10).

THE PROBLEM

Rome demanded faithfulness to a commitment on the part of those who served as tax collectors. That Zacchaeus was continued in that office by Rome was an evidence of his faithfulness to Rome in the discharge of his office. Since the disciples understood that Rome required a commitment from people like Zacchaeus, the question would quite naturally arise as to what Christ expected of those who had made a commitment to Him.

THE SOLUTION

In order to answer this question, Christ told the parable of the ten minas. It was especially important that the disciples understand what was expected of them in view of the postponement of the Davidic kingdom. Christ knew that "the people thought that the kingdom of God was going to appear at once" (Luke 19:11). To stress the fact that the kingdom was being postponed, Christ said, "A man of noble birth went to a distant country to have himself appointed king and then to return" (v. 12). In the story Christ may well have had a historical incident in mind, for Archelaus, the son of Herod the Great, had gone to Rome after his father's death to be confirmed as ruler in Judea and Samaria. His brother Antipas had also gone to Rome seeking the same appointment. Since the Jews hated Archelaus, they lodged a protest with the emperor against his appointment; but in spite of it, Archelaus was appointed ruler of Judea and Samaria by the emperor. This well-known historical incident must have created great interest on the part of Jesus' hearers as to what He was teaching. Since the nobleman anticipated an extended absence, he called ten of his servants and gave to each one a mina. A mina was one's wages for approximately three months; so this was a considerable sum. The servants were held responsible as stewards

for the use of the money entrusted to them. During the nobleman's absence, a protest objecting to his appointment was lodged
by his subjects with the one who had the authority to confirm
him as king. Such a rejection of the nobleman would test the
loyalty and faithfulness of his stewards on whom he had conferred
this responsibility of stewardship.

In this part of the parable, Christ was likening Himself to the
nobleman who had gone to a distant country. Christ was returning to His Father because of the rejection of Himself as Messiah
and of His kingdom. During his absence He would confer a
responsibility on His servants. Although there would be continuing opposition to Him, He expected those whom He had
appointed to be loyal and faithful.

The king in Christ's parable returned after his confirmation
despite the objection of those over whom he would rule. The
servants were called to give an account of their stewardship.
Some of the servants were found faithful. One's mina had been
used to gain ten minas, and another's had gained five. The king
appointed the faithful to positions of administrative authority in
his kingdom (cf. Matt. 19:28–30).

In contrast, there was a servant who was found faithless. This
servant's mina was not used to benefit the nobleman, and in fact
nothing had been done with it. The servant could only return the
mina to the nobleman with a confession of acting out of fear.
Without doubt, this servant had joined in the opposition against
the confirmation of the nobleman as king. This rejection of the
nobleman had led to unfaithfulness. The servant's unfaithfulness
was a reflection of a rebellious attitude toward the nobleman,
who had trusted the servant as evidenced by his assignment concerning the mina. As a judgment the servant's stewardship of the
mina was then taken away and entrusted to one who had proven
faithful. The severity of the judgment is seen in the king's command: "But those enemies of mine who did not want me to be
king over them—bring them here and kill them in front of me"
(Luke 19:27). The unfaithful were removed from the kingdom
over which the king ruled. In this part of the parable Christ was

viewing the nation of Israel as His stewards. They had originally been chosen by God for special service (Exod. 19:6). As a kingdom of priests they were to receive revelation from God and disseminate it to those in spiritual darkness. Moses was commanded to place a lampstand in the holy place of the tabernacle as a perpetual reminder that God had chosen Israel to be light to the world. God had promised to raise up a King in David's line to rule over David's people (2 Sam. 7:16), and the prophets had anticipated the coming of that King. When Christ came and was introduced by John as the King, the people professed to welcome Him. But when Christ offered Himself and spelled out the requirements for entrance into His kingdom (Matt. 5:48), they turned aside from Him; and the leaders of the nation registered their rejection of Christ (12:24). God had revealed Himself through the Law and through the Prophets, and that revelation was a stewardship for which the nation was responsible. Because the nation rejected Him, Christ returned to the Father in order to be confirmed as King by Him. The words with which the Father welcomed the Son into glory after His ascension are found in Psalm 110:1–2: "The LORD says to my Lord: 'Sit at my right hand until I make your enemies a footstool for your feet.' The LORD will extend your mighty scepter from Zion; rule in the midst of your enemies." In view of Christ's absence a stewardship has been entrusted to His disciples who are expected to be loyal and faithful. At the time of the King's return to assume the prerogatives of kingship, the stewards will be tested. The faithful will be received into the kingdom that the King establishes, and the unfaithful will be rejected. Faithfulness springs from faith in the person of the King, and unfaithfulness is the result of the rejection of the King.

Thus Christ answered the question of what is expected of disciples. They are to be loyal and faithful.

THE TWO SONS
Matthew 21:28–32

THE SETTING

The preceding context concerns an occasion when Christ went into the temple courts and was challenged by the priests and the elders (Matt. 21:23–27). The issue was the authority by which He had assumed the role of Messiah and had presented Himself as Messiah in the triumphal entry and in cleansing the temple. Since these acts were clearly in fulfillment of messianic prophecies, the leaders questioned Christ's right to pose as Messiah. Christ raised a question concerning the ministry of John, whom the common people held to be a prophet from God. The inference was that Christ had the same authority as John had. The leaders were afraid to reply, for either they would offend the people who believed that John was a prophet, or they would place themselves under an obligation to submit to the authority of John and Jesus, which they refused to do. John demanded that the people confess that they were sinners and in need of salvation. In contrast, the religious leaders affirmed that they were righteous and needed no repentance; and they considered themselves to be sons of the kingdom.

THE PROBLEM

As a result of the conflict in claims between Christ and the Jewish leaders, two questions arose: "Who is a son of the kingdom? How may sonship be tested?" These were crucial questions, for their answers would determine whether or not those who followed Pharisaic traditions were accepted by God.

THE SOLUTION

Christ told of a man who had two sons. The father, as he had a right to do, commanded his first son to go and work in the vineyard. The son deliberately refused to do this, saying, "I will not" (Matt. 21:29a). By refusing the son was repudiating his

133

father's rightful authority. In the parable Christ added, "But later he changed his mind and went" (v. 29b). Now the son was submitting to his father's authority. Thus in spite of speaking words that disavowed his father's authority, by his act of obedience he was showing submission to his father's authority. Later, the father commanded his second son to go and work in the vineyard alongside the first son, who had shown obedience to the father. The second son said, "I will, sir" (v. 30). By his words he was professing to recognize the father's authority; however, "he did not go." In spite of his profession he refused to submit to his father. Christ then asked, "Which of the two did what his father wanted?" (v. 31). The only logical answer that the Jewish leaders could give was "The first." Thus in the parable Christ was showing that profession of obedience does not constitute sonship. Sonship is tested by obedience, not by profession. Thus the Pharisees who claimed to be sons of God but did not obey the law and fulfill its righteousness could not be counted as sons. But one who submitted to the authority of the law and obeyed it was a son. This test would exclude the leaders who were challenging Christ from participation in His kingdom. The leaders would never have accepted tax collectors and prostitutes as being eligible to enter the kingdom, let alone actually be in it. But Christ affirmed that those who received John's message in faith were acceptable to God and were actually in the kingdom. Thus Christ disproved the claim of the leaders that they needed no repentance because they were already sons of the kingdom.

THE OWNER OF A VINEYARD
Matthew 21:33–44

THE SETTING

The words that introduce this section, "Listen to another parable" (Matt. 21:33), show that Christ was continuing the teaching contained in the parable of the two sons concerning the Pharisees and their relationship to His kingdom.

THE PROBLEM

Since the nation of Israel, under the leadership of their religious authority, was rejecting Christ, two questions arose: What would happen to that nation? What would be the course of the kingdom in view of that rejection?

THE SOLUTION

The background of this parable is found in Isaiah 5 where the prophet described a vineyard that had been planted "on a fertile hillside" (v. 1) and that gave every prospect of producing a bountiful harvest. The person who planted the vineyard had carefully prepared the soil to receive the vine. He had "dug it up and cleared it of stones" (v. 2) to remove every obstacle to the growth of the vine. A watchtower for protection had been built, and a wine press had been provided in anticipation of the harvest. But when the time of harvest came, the vine yielded only "bad [literally, rotten or stinking] fruit" (v. 2). This quite obviously was a parable, and the prophet now proceeded with the explanation. God had planted the vineyard, and the nation of Israel was His choice vine (v. 3). He had brought them out of the desert and into a good land. He had protected them in the land, and He had anticipated that He would receive good fruit from them. The kind of fruit God saw is explained in verse 7: "He looked for justice, but saw bloodshed; for righteousness, but heard cries of distress [or rebellion]." Thus the nation of Israel had not walked righteously and justly before God. In His parable Christ used the

135

same imagery as the prophet. Christ was reviewing the history of the nation. They had been planted in a good land. God had provided protection by giving them the law, and He anticipated the fruit of righteousness from the people. The vineyard was then rented to farmers who were responsible for cultivating, pruning, and tending the vine so that it would produce a bountiful harvest. The farmers represented the leaders in the nation who in past generations had exercised authority over the people.

Christ said that at the time of the harvest servants were sent to collect fruit. The servants represented the prophets whom God had sent during Israel's history to call the people to repentance and obedience and to encourage the people to demonstrate righteousness. However, those who had authority over the vineyard rejected the servants. "They beat one, killed another, and stoned a third" (Matt. 21:35). In an unusual display of patience, the owner did not remove the tenants but instead sent additional servants to receive the fruit of the harvest. However, the leaders responded to these servants the same way. Thus Christ indicated how Israel had treated God's prophets. In a display of grace, instead of bringing judgment on the leaders, the owner provided one more opportunity for the tenants to produce fruit. This time he sent his son to them, saying, "They will respect my son" (v. 37). In this parable the son is a clear reference to Christ Himself. Thus Christ revealed that He had come to do what the prophets in previous generations had tried to do. Christ came to call the people to repentance, to invoke obedience, and to produce righteousness in the nation so as to please God. However, the leaders conspired to kill the son. They repudiated the owner's right to rule and assumed that authority for themselves. Christ thus was anticipating His ultimate rejection and death. The Lord then asked, "What will he (the owner) do to those tenants?" (Matt. 21:40). The only logical answer was that the owner would exercise his authority to remove those who misused the oversight entrusted to them. The owner would appoint other overseers who would produce the harvest that rightly belonged to the owner (v. 41). Those who gave this reply were actually passing judgment on themselves. Having failed to see how the parable involved them, they showed themselves to be worthy of being removed from positions of authority in the nation. Christ showed by referring to Psalm 118:22–23 that this process of rejection was in keeping with the prophetic Scriptures.

Christ then revealed the judgment that would come on that generation and their leaders, who had rejected every exhortation through the prophets and were now not only rejecting the exhortation of Christ but were in the process of putting Him to death. Christ said, "The kingdom of God will be taken away from you and given to a people who will produce its fruit" (Matt. 21:43). There had been different ways in which the theocracy had been administered in the Old Testament prior to the announcement of the covenanted form of the theocracy to be administered through a Davidic descendant (2 Sam. 7:16). Now Christ revealed that the theocracy, which in its millennial form had been offered to that generation, would be taken from them and given to a people who would produce its fruit. The identity of "a people" in Matthew 21:43 has been variously interpreted. Some have seen this as an indication that the theocracy will be given to a future generation in the nation of Israel. This will be done during the Tribulation period prior to the second advent of Christ, at which time the gospel of the kingdom will be preached again (Matt. 24:14). Others see "a people" as a reference to the Gentiles who will be the people through whom God works during the period in which Israel is set aside. This would be in keeping with James' statement at the Jerusalem council: "Brothers, listen to me. Simon has described to us how God at first showed his concern by taking from the Gentiles a people for himself" (Acts. 15:13–14). This would be the basis for Paul's doctrine (Eph. 2–3). The middle wall of partition has been broken down between Jew and Gentile, and from the two God at the present time is making a people for His name. With either interpretation, it is evident that God has withdrawn the privileges offered to that generation with respect to entering into the full benefits of the covenanted and promised kingdom. When Christ said, "He on whom it [this stone] falls will be crushed" (Matt. 21:44), He was anticipating the coming judgment on that generation that would be consummated through Titus' invasion in A.D. 70. The alternative to such a judgment is given in the clause "He who falls on this stone," meaning the one who casts oneself in faith on Jesus Christ will escape the judgment and will be received into the kingdom.

Both the chief priests and Pharisees understood the parable. They realized that Christ was speaking of them as the tenants of the vineyard whom He had deemed to be faithless and on whom He had passed this severe judgment. They wanted to arrest and kill Christ at that time but were afraid to do so because the people counted Him as He had pictured Himself in the parable, a Prophet from God.

THE WEDDING BANQUET
Matthew 22:1–14

THE SETTING

During this period in His ministry Christ had to face the reality of His rejection even though the covenanted kingdom had been offered and that offer adequately authenticated by both His words and works. The leaders influenced the nation to reject both Christ's person and offer. As a consequence Christ was no longer publicly offering the kingdom but was announcing its postponement and telling of the severe judgment that was to fall on the nation.

THE PROBLEM

The question persisted as to what would happen to the generation that was guilty of the sin of rejecting Christ. Another question was, Who will be accepted into the kingdom that will be instituted after the time of the postponement has passed?

THE SOLUTION

Christ had addressed Himself previously to such questions (Matt. 21:33–45). Now He once again gave an answer in the parable of the king who prepared a wedding banquet. Christ was using familiar Oriental wedding customs to teach an important lesson. At the time of the betrothal an announcement was sent to the bridegroom's friends to inform them of the forthcoming wedding, and the friends were invited to attend the wedding banquet that would follow. Customarily, twelve months intervened between the betrothal and the wedding itself; therefore, the invited guests had had ample opportunity to prepare themselves to attend the wedding banquet. In His parable Christ commenced the story when the king, the father of the bridegroom, "sent his servants to those who had been invited to the banquet to tell them to come" (Matt. 22:3). This would have been the second invitation, since

139

the first invitation was given at the time of the betrothal. Thus it was sent out to those who had previously been invited. This second invitation announced the date for the wedding and the wedding banquet. Now the guests were expected to attend the wedding banquet. In Christ's symbolism of the parable, those who had been invited refer to the nation with which God had made a covenant, promising them a Messiah who would institute the kingdom of peace and righteousness in which they were privileged to have a part. The response of the guests to this second invitation was quite unexpected, for "they refused to come" (v. 3).

The graciousness of the host is seen in the fact that he considered the possibility that the invited guests may not have understood the urgency of the second invitation. The host graciously sent more servants to inform the invited guests that the dinner had been prepared. The servants, indeed, made the banquet most attractive, for they informed the prospective guests that those who came would dine sumptuously on oxen and cattle that had been fattened to provide food for the banquet. And the invitation was pressed on the guests with the servants urging, "Come to the wedding banquet" (v. 4). It was indeed gracious of the host to extend these additional invitations and to make every effort to make the banquet attractive, for in the light of their rejection he was under no obligation to them. In this part of the parable, Christ was reminding His hearers that God spoke through the prophets and invited the nation to prepare to enter the kingdom. When John the Baptist began his ministry, he announced that the kingdom was at hand. Christ reiterated the announcement of John and urged those who had been invited and who had been told that the banquet was ready to attend the banquet, that is, to enter the promised kingdom. But Israel as a nation refused to do so.

The parable suggests reasons for Israel's failure to respond to the invitation. The invited guests were preoccupied with their own affairs. One guest was concerned with his field. He was laboring to increase his own wealth and ignored the invitation in order to guarantee a good harvest. Another guest, in like manner, devoted himself to his business. He did not want to interrupt his business to attend the wedding banquet, lest through neglect he lose some of the benefits that he expected to obtain. Thus we see that preoccupation with the pursuit of material things prevented these people from heeding the invitation to attend the banquet. Some who received invitations used violence to remove any further pressure to attend the banquet; they mistreated and killed the servants who were urging them to attend. In this part of the parable Christ was referring to the death of John and to His own approaching death as indicating Israel's rejection of the kingdom that had been offered.

The parable goes on to give the response of the king to the rejection. The first result of the rejection was that the king "sent his army and destroyed those murderers and burned their city" (Matt. 22:7). The king recognized that the refusal to respond to the invitation was a rejection of him and evidence of disrespect for his person. Therefore, he meted out a severe judgment on them. Not only were the rebels destroyed, but their city was burned. Again, Christ was anticipating the divine judgment that would fall on Jerusalem in A.D. 70, at which time Titus destroyed the city and killed 1.5 million inhabitants of the land in his conquest.

But a second result of the rejection of Christ by the generation of Jews of His day was that a new invitation was extended. It was inconceivable to the host that there would be empty places at the wedding banquet. Therefore, the host's servants were commanded, "Go to the street corners and invite to the banquet anyone you find" (v. 8). Apparently Christ was indicating that an invitation would be given to the people in that nation to enter the new form of the theocracy that would be instituted following His death and resurrection. The Book of Acts records that in the decade following the death of Christ the message of the gospel went primarily to the Jews. The apostles were commanded to be witnesses for Christ first in Jerusalem and Judea where Jews lived (Acts. 1:8). The parable indicates that through this invitation "the wedding hall was filled with guests" (v. 10). This also seems to indicate that the message will again be brought to the nation that had first rejected the invitation. Through the preaching of the "gospel of the kingdom" (Matt. 24:14), the nation again will be invited to enter the coming millennial form of the kingdom. This invitation will be extended to Israel during the seven years of the Tribulation that will follow the Rapture and that will be prior to the second advent of Christ to the earth.

As Christ concluded this parable, He taught again that only those who are prepared will enter any future form of the theocracy. He said that when the king came to the wedding banquet and looked over the guests, "he noticed a man there who was not wearing wedding clothes" (22:11). The man was unprepared to attend the wedding banquet. Since the invitation had been extended a considerable time before the banquet was actually to be held, the man had had an ample opportunity to obtain the clothing that was expected of wedding guests. This one wanted to enjoy the delights of the banquet but had come unprepared. When he was questioned as to why he was unprepared, he had no answer. He had known what was expected. He had had an opportunity to secure the proper clothes, but he had not done so. It may be that he thought that the host would be honored to have him attend even though he was unprepared. He may have concluded that such clothes as he already had were sufficient for the wedding. However, the host judged otherwise and commanded, "Tie him hand and foot, and throw him outside, into the darkness, where there will be weeping and gnashing of teeth" (v. 13). Christ was again giving instructions to those who considered themselves to be righteous and acceptable to God and who saw themselves as members of His kingdom. Christ revealed that unless they prepared themselves to be judged acceptable by the host, they would be excluded from the kingdom when it was instituted. Christ's closing word was "For many are invited, but few are chosen" (v. 14); by this He indicated that not all who have been invited will participate in the kingdom. Christ was teaching that it was not enough to just be a member of the covenanted nation; not all Israelites related to Abraham by blood would be included in Christ's millennial reign. Rather, only those who heard the invitation and then prepared themselves would have their part in Messiah's kingdom.

THE FIG TREE
Matthew 24:32-34

THE SETTING

After pronouncing woes on the Pharisees, Christ once again had announced the forthcoming judgment on Jerusalem (Matt. 23:37–39). In response to the consternation of the disciples, He had explained, "Not one stone here will be left on another; every one will be thrown down" (24:2). Without the city of Jerusalem and the temple, there could be no national life for Israel. The attention of the Lord's Jewish hearers must have turned to the prophecy in Zechariah 12:1–14:3 that foretells the destruction of Jerusalem by Gentile powers prior to Messiah's advent to the earth to institute His millennial kingdom (14:4). If so, this would explain the reason for the disciples' question, "When will this happen, and what will be the sign of your coming and of the end of the age?" (Matt. 24:3). The disciples were concerned with the signs that would fall in the seven years of the Tribulation that which Israel was waiting for the coming Messiah and His messianic kingdom and of the beginning of the new age to be instituted by Messiah at His coming. In response Christ outlined the signs that would fall in the seven years of the tribulation that would precede Christ's second advent (Matt. 24:4–26; cf. Dan. 9:24–27). The lord first referred to the signs falling in the first half of the Tribulation (Matt. 24:4–8). He said, "All these are the beginning of birth pains" (v. 8). Then Christ spoke of signs occurring in the second half of the Tribulation (vv. 9–14).

Christ also described the principal sign that will be given to the nation, that is, "the abomination that causes desolation, spoken of through the prophet Daniel" (v. 15).

In verses 26–30 Christ described "the coming of the Son of Man"; and He warned the nation that just as vultures settle on a dead carcass, so He will come the second time as a Judge. He forewarned the nation of His coming as Judge in order that they might prepare themselves for His judgment when He would come "with power and great glory" (v. 30).

Following the second advent of Christ, the nation of Israel, referred to here as "his elect" because He had chosen them and entered into covenant with them, will be regathered "from one end of the heavens to the other" (v. 31).

THE PROBLEM

Two main questions would have arisen in the minds of those who heard the details of this discourse: What is the significance of these signs? What should be the reaction of those who see these signs to the signs themselves?

THE SOLUTION

In order to answer these important questions, Christ drew a lesson from nature. Matthew quoted, "Now learn this lesson from the fig tree" (v. 32). Luke expanded the imagery, quoting, "Look at the fig tree and all the trees" (Luke 21:29). Thus Christ was not calling attention to just the fig tree itself (as though the fig tree represented the nation of Israel, as has been quite commonly inferred). Rather, Christ was calling attention to a truth that was pictured by something that characterizes all trees. There was, then, a general principle that Christ wanted His hearers to observe. During the winter months the trees were bare. People who had endured the long, cold, damp winter were looking forward to the coming of summer. As they walked along a path, they would see the first tender green shoot on a fig tree, or on any tree. This green growth was a sign to them that what they were longing for, and what they knew eventually would come, was not far off. A process had begun that would eventuate in summer. This universal principle was applied by Christ when He said, "Even so, when you see all these things, you know that it [or better, He] is near, right at the door" (Matt. 24:33). By "these things" Christ was referring to all the signs given in verses 4–26. Christ was saying that the appearance of the first of these signs would serve notice to Israel that Messiah was coming. The sign would serve notice of

His coming in the way that the first green shoot serves notice to those that have endured the long winter that spring is on the way. Christ then added, "This generation will certainly not pass away until all these things have happened" (v. 34). By "this generation" Christ meant the generation in Israel that would see the signs given in verses 4–26. These same signs are discussed in more detail in Revelation 4–19. These signs all fall within the seventieth week of Daniel's prophecy (Dan. 9:27) and consequently will be fulfilled within a seven-year period. Since the program from its inception to its consummation will transpire in so brief a period of time, those who see the first signs also will see the completion of the program. They are those referred to in verse 34.

It is an improper interpretation of this parable to insist that the fig tree represents the nation of Israel and that the budding of the fig tree represents the reinstitution of the national life of that people in 1948. Likewise, it is incorrect to conclude that within a generation following 1948 the Second Advent must take place. While this is currently a popular view, it is not based on a sound interpretation of the passage. This view would make the parable applicable to the church and the signs would be given to the church. However the signs were given to Israel and are applicable to that nation.

THE KEEPER OF THE DOOR
Mark 13:33–37

THE SETTING

In the light of the promise of His coming given in the Olivet Discourse, the Lord gave exhortations to watchfulness. He commanded, "Be on guard! Be alert!" (Mark 13:33).

THE PROBLEM

The question would then arise, Why should one be alert?

THE SOLUTION

The fulfillment of the signs preceding the coming of Christ (Matt. 24:4–26) will reveal that those seeing the signs are living in the last days, or in the time of the end. However, those who see the signs will not be able to determine the actual date of Christ's coming. Daniel 9:27 indicates that the time of Jacob's trouble (Jer. 30:7)—the Tribulation—will be seven years in duration. Elsewhere, this period is given in months and even in days (Rev. 11:2–3). One might ask why people will not know the day or the hour when the time is so clearly stated. Perhaps the reason is that the people will not be able to determine the actual inception of this significant prophetic period. Daniel 9:27 reveals that the period will begin when the little horn (Dan. 7:8), who is also called the Beast (Rev. 13:1), makes a covenant with the nation of Israel. Normally it takes some time to explore the possibilities of a covenant, formalize the covenant, attain agreement on the terms of the covenant and consent to the covenant, and then to actually inaugurate the covenant. The individuals living through that period will not know when during that process the seven years of the Tribulation actually commenced. Thus while they will know they are living in the last days and that the coming of Christ is near, they will not be able to determine the actual day or the hour. In the light of the uncertainty of the actual time of

147

Christ's coming, those who will be expecting Him momentarily should be on guard and alert.

When the owner of a house plans for his absence, he commits responsibilities to his servants that are to be performed while he is away; consequently, the servants are not under his direct supervision. The owner expects faithfulness on the part of the servants even though he is absent from them. If the servant's responsibility is to guard the gate, the servant must discharge that job faithfully. The servant must not neglect an assigned post, for the owner might return any time (Matt. 13:35). If the servant reasoned that the owner would not return immediately and the servant forsook an assigned post, the owner might well return during the absence of the servant, who then would be found derelict in obedience. Therefore, if the servant is to prove faithful, that servant must be on the job and be awake and watching.

Thus Christ's promise of an imminent return was designed to produce faithfulness in His servants.

THE WATCHFUL OWNER AND THE WISE SERVANT
Matthew 24:42-51

THE SETTING

In the course of giving His Olivet Discourse, Christ was instructing His hearers concerning the uncertainty of the time of His return. The signs given in Matthew 24:4-26 would alert the nation to the fact that they were living in the last days. However, "no one knows about that day or hour, not even the angels in heaven, nor the Son, but only the Father" (v. 36). Christ likened those days immediately preceding His second advent to the days of Noah. Noah forewarned his generation of an impending judgment that was to come through the Flood. The message was clearly understood, but it was ignored. The people occupied themselves with the normal activities of life, eating and drinking, and marrying and giving in marriage. There was nothing morally wrong with living in a normal way, but they were living joyously when they should have been preparing for judgment. Christ revealed that when the signs of Messiah's approach are given in the last days, the generation that sees those signs will act like Noah's generation, that is, they will ignore them and go on with the normal way of life.

THE PROBLEM

Christ faced the question of how those who witnessed the signs should respond to them. One reason for giving signs was to alert people so they could prepare themselves for the judgment that would follow Christ's appearance. Christ spoke of this judgment when He said, "Two men will be in the field; one will be taken [away in judgment] and the other left [to go into the kingdom]. Two women will be grinding with a hand mill; one will be taken [away in judgment] and the other left [to go into the millennial kingdom]" (Matt. 24:40-41).

149

The Solution

In order to answer the question, Christ gave two brief parables to teach watchfulness, preparedness, and faithfulness. The first parable concerns the owner of a house who received information that a thief was coming (Matt. 24:42–44). He was forewarned not only of the fact, but even was given the time at which the thief would attempt to enter the home. Christ's emphasis here was on the forewarning that the owner of the household had been given. In view of this warning, the owner would prepare for the coming of the thief by setting a watch; through this preparation the owner would prevent his house from being broken into. The application intended by Christ was that those who see the sign would have a warning of the approaching advent of Christ. Having been warned, they should prepare themselves for His coming even as the owner of the house had prepared for the thief's coming. If they refused to be watchful and chose to neglect the warning they had received, then they would be carried away in the judgment that Messiah will mete out at His coming. Thus in the first parable Christ's answer was to stress watchfulness and preparedness.

In the second parable Christ stressed the need for faithfulness on the part of those who will witness the signs (Matt. 24:45–51). The Lord referred to a master who before his departure gave instructions to a servant under his authority. A servant was expected to faithfully do the assignments that were given. When the master returned, he would note the faithfulness of his servant. If a servant was found faithful, that servant would be given added responsibilities. Thus the parable instructed those who will witness the signs that they should be diligent, even though the Lord is absent, so that when He comes they might be found faithful and therefore receive a reward.

It would be possible for the servant mentioned above to become lax during the master's absence. The servant could misuse the authority that had been delegated by the master and start mistreating other servants instead of supervising them. Instead of discharging the assigned responsibilities, a servant might use the time of the master's absence for self-indulgence. Such a foolish servant would continue a faithless course of conduct, not knowing when the master would return. But when the master returned and discovered the conduct of his servant, the master would "cut him to pieces and assign him a place with the hypocrites, where there will be weeping and gnashing of teeth" (Matt. 24:51). In this portion of the parable Christ was revealing that if people are unfaithful to the stewardship entrusted to them, and if they ignore the signs that will be given of the return of the Lord, they will be kept from the kingdom to be established at His coming. In these parables the servants represent the people of the nation of Israel who will be God's stewards during the Tribulation. At Christ's return the nation will be judged, the faithful will be received into the kingdom, and the unfaithful will be excluded from the kingdom. Here again the faithfulness is that which springs from faith in Christ, while the unfaithfulness is produced because of lack of faith in Christ. Thus in view of the signs given to Israel, the people are exhorted to be watchful, prepared, and faithful. The reason is that the signs indicate the coming of a Judge who will separate the saved from the unsaved.

THE TEN VIRGINS
Matthew 25:1–13

THE SETTING

Christ in the Olivet Discourse began by moving in a strictly chronological sequence through the eschatological program for the nation of Israel. In Matthew 24:4–26 He covered the seven years of the Tribulation, also called the time of Jacob's trouble (Jer. 30:7). He next described His second advent to the earth (vv. 27–30), followed by the regathering of the nation of Israel back to the land. We next find a parentheses in the chronology of events in which Christ gave exhortations through parables to watchfulness, preparedness, and faithfulness (vv. 32–51). Then in two parables Christ described the next eschatological event in the program for Israel following the Second Advent, namely, judgment on living Israel in order to separate the saved from the unsaved (25:1–30). The phrase "at that time" (v. 1) is to be connected sequentially to 24:31.

THE PROBLEM

In the context that immediately precedes (Matt. 24:50–51), Christ had spoken of a judgment that would exclude unprepared Israelites from Messiah's kingdom. A question then arose concerning this judgment: On what ground would the nation be judged?

THE SOLUTION

Christ's answer to this question is given first in the parable of the ten virgins (Matt. 25:1–13). The context must be noted at the outset. Christ was dealing here with judgment for the nation of Israel. The church is not in view anywhere in the discourse of Matthew 24–25. Rather, Christ was developing the eschatology of the nation of Israel. Although Paul did refer to the church as a "pure virgin" (2 Cor. 11:2), his use of the similar figure with reference to the church does not prove that the church is in view

152

in this parable. Once again Christ was using the familiar figure of the Oriental wedding customs. A second invitation had been sent to those previously invited, notifying them that the wedding banquet had been prepared and they were expected to attend. The bridegroom had left his father's home to go to the bride's home in order to claim the girl who had been betrothed to him. According to custom, the bride's father would prepare a banquet for his daughter and invite her friends so that she might celebrate the forthcoming wedding with them. How long the banqueting in the bride's home might last was unknown. Therefore, as the invited guests assembled for the wedding banquet in the bridegroom's home, they expected to wait for an indeterminate period before the bridegroom came to the banquet with his bride. The ten virgins had assembled at the place where the wedding banquet would be spread, and they were also awaiting the appearance of the bridegroom with his bride.

The ten virgins were divided into two classes, the foolish and the wise. The foolish ones had made no provision for an extension of the bridegroom's delay. Since the lamps could hold only a small amount of oil, it was customary to carry extra oil in a jar so that the lamps could be replenished from this supply. The wise, recognizing the possibility of delay, had taken extra oil in jars. Then when there was a delay, they could replenish the oil in their lamps and thus keep their lamps burning.

When night fell those awaiting the banquet had concluded that the bridegroom would wait until daylight to travel. But contrary to custom, the bridegroom had left the bride's home and traveled after dark. He had arrived at his home village around midnight. Since the guests had not expected the bridegroom, they had all gone to sleep. When the bridegroom approached the outskirts of his village, he sent word ahead of his arrival so that those who had assembled for the banquet might go out to meet him. They could then accompany the bridegroom and bride to the place where the banquet would be held. It was after dark, and so one could not go out to meet the bridegroom without a lamp. This circumstance brought out clearly the difference between the two classes of virgins. The wise virgins were able to fill their lamps and go to meet the bridegroom, whereas the foolish virgins had no oil in reserve and were unable to meet the bridegroom. Thus some were prepared for the delay, while others were unprepared.

The unprepared wanted to meet the bridegroom and his bride so as to be included in the wedding banquet. They sought to obtain oil. Since it was impossible to purchase oil in the market at that hour, they sought to borrow some from the virgins who had prepared for the bridegroom's delay. However, the wise refused to share their oil. The wise virgins were not selfish but rather they were faithful to the bridegroom. They desired to go and meet him and they needed their oil to be able to join the procession to the banquet hall. The parable points out that those "who were ready went in with him to the wedding banquet. And the door was shut" (Matt. 25:10).

The unprepared virgins had no choice but to wait and then obtain oil when the market opened at daybreak. After purchasing a supply, they presented themselves at the banquet hall and asked to be admitted. But the host refused to open the door.

Although a strong testimony will be given to the nation of Israel during the Tribulation (Matt. 24:14), some people will be unprepared when the King comes to institute His millennial kingdom. The prepared will be received into the kingdom to enjoy its bounty but the unprepared will be excluded. Thus this parable teaches that there will be a judgment of living Israelites to determine who is and is not prepared. This is an expansion of Christ's previous statement that "you also must be ready" (Matt. 24:44).

THE TALENTS
Matthew 25:14–30

THE SETTING

Prior to speaking this parable, Christ had instructed His listeners concerning faithfulness (Matt. 24:45–51).

THE PROBLEM

Christ now discussed the importance of being found faithful at His coming. He answered the following question: What judgment will be meted out to those who are unfaithful?

THE SOLUTION

This question finds its answer in the parable of the talents, which in many ways is similar to the parable of the ten minas (cf. Luke 19:11–27). In that parable ten servants were each given a mina, and thus the stress was on equal opportunity. In this parable the emphasis is on individual responsibility. A man going on a journey called his servants and gave five talents to one, two to another, and one to a third. In that day a talent was a very large sum of money; so this parable stresses the great responsibility placed on each servant. Having distributed the talents, the master then went on his journey with the expectation that the servants would be faithful to the trust he had given them during his absence. When the master eventually returned, he called his servants to give an account of their stewardship. Two of the servants were found to be faithful because both had doubled their talents. The master rewarded them for their faithfulness, saying to each servant, "Well done, good and faithful servant! You have been faithful with a few things; I will put you in charge of many things. Come and share your master's happiness!" (Matt. 25:21; cf. v. 23). It is interesting that even though the amount of money entrusted to them was great in the world's eyes, it was counted by the master as "a few things." The two had exercised their respon-

155

sibilities faithfully and were to be appointed to greater positions of responsibility in the administration of their master's affairs. Christ was revealing the high value He puts on faithfulness on the part of those waiting for the Lord's return. Those who wait faithfully not only will be received into Messiah's kingdom but will be given responsibilities in the kingdom.

Christ now proceeded in the parable to show the results of unfaithfulness. The man who had received the one talent returned what had been entrusted to him; however, out of fear for his master, this servant had done nothing with the one talent in his care. Since he had had the opportunity to multiply his master's goods but had not done so, he had proved himself unfaithful. Therefore, the master said, "You wicked, lazy servant! . . . Take the talent from him and give it to the one who has the ten talents. . . . And throw that worthless servant outside, into the darkness, where there will be weeping and gnashing of teeth" (Matt. 25:26–30). The unfaithful servant not only failed to receive a reward but was completely excluded from his master's household. In this parable Christ was teaching that those who see the signs forewarning of Messiah's approach will have an opportunity to prepare themselves and to prove themselves faithful servants of His; however, if such persons do not do so, they will be barred from the kingdom that Christ will establish at His second coming. The parable, then, shows both the rewards for faithfulness and the judgment for unfaithfulness that await those who are anticipating Messiah's coming.

THE SHEEP AND THE GOATS
Matthew 25:31-46

THE SETTING

Thus far in the Olivet Discourse Christ had been unfolding the chronology of eschatological events for the nation of Israel. The Davidic kingdom to be established at the second advent of Christ is certainly Israel's kingdom. However, the Old Testament has made it clear that Gentiles will have their part in that kingdom. For example, God promised Abram, "All people on earth will be blessed through you" (Gen. 12:3). The prophets had predicted the blessing that would come on Gentiles when Messiah establishes His kingdom with them (Zech. 8:20-23).

THE PROBLEM

In the light of this, the question arose as to the basis on which Gentiles would be included in the millennial kingdom.

THE SOLUTION

In the parable of the sheep and goats, Christ revealed the judgment that will come on living Gentiles following Israel's judgment. The parable discloses who from among the Gentiles will enter the millennial kingdom and who will be excluded. At the outset Christ described the glory that will be His when He comes to earth the second time. The Lord referred to Himself as "the Son of Man" (Matt. 25:31), the title He most frequently used for Himself during His earthly ministry and one that from the time of its first use in Daniel 7:13 was considered a messianic title. Christ also spoke of the "throne" on which He will sit; namely, the Davidic throne that He will occupy as David's descendant when He rules over David's kingdom (2 Sam. 7:16; Luke 1:32-33). The same glory that Peter, James, and John saw on the Mount of Transfiguration and that was a preview of the millennial glory of Christ (Matt. 17:1-2) will be revealed to the

157

world at Christ's second advent. When the Lord returns, He will gather all nations before Him. The Greek word translated "nations" (25:32) is most frequently translated "Gentiles" (4:15; 10:5 et al.). The Gentiles will be brought together for judgment, not as national entities but rather as individuals. This part of the parable views Israel as already judged, as well as "all the Gentiles" (v. 32); therefore, no living individual will be exempted from judgment prior to the actual establishment of the millennial kingdom. As a shepherd would separate sheep from goats, so Christ will divide into two groups all who appear before Him at this judgment. "He will put the sheep on his right and the goats on his left" (v. 33).

The Judge at this judgment is referred to as "the King" (v. 34), emphasizing that the One who will reign is the One who will judge. The King describes those on the right hand as "blessed by my Father" and commands them, "Take your inheritance, the kingdom prepared for you since the creation of the world." They are to experience the blessings of the King's reign in His kingdom. The basis for the invitation to enter the kingdom is now given: "For I was hungry and you gave me something to eat, I was thirsty and you gave me something to drink, I was a stranger and you invited me in, I needed clothes and you clothed me, I was sick and you looked after me, I was in prison and you came to visit me" (vv. 35–36). Those invited into the kingdom will then protest that it was impossible for them to have done those things inasmuch as they had never seen the Lord before.

He will reply, "Whatever you did for one of the least of these brothers of mine, you did for me" (v. 40). By this statement in verse 40 Christ will refer to a third group there in His presence as King. They are "these brothers of mine." Several explanations have been offered to identify these brothers. Since the nation of Israel will have been judged previously, and the wise and the faithful will have been admitted into the kingdom, some have suggested that the brothers represent believers in the nation of Israel. Others have noted that God will seal 144,000 from among the tribes of Israel to become His servants (Rev. 7:1–8) and that this group will proclaim the gospel of salvation by grace through faith in the blood of Christ (v. 14) throughout the Tribulation. On this basis these witnesses are thought to be represented by the "brothers" in Matthew 25:40. This interpretation, perhaps, is best. These servants will minister during the rule of the Beast (Rev. 13:1–2), whose desire will be to exterminate the nation of Israel (v. 7). These witnesses will be targets of the Beast's hatred. Since they will refuse to submit to his authority, many of them will be hungry and thirsty, without clothing, and even imprisoned because of their devotion to Christ. There will be those who will hear and believe God's message for that day and who will practice their faith despite the danger that they will incur. These "brothers" will feed, clothe, and extend hospitality to those whom the Beast will seek to kill. They will aid the messengers because they believe the message. Christ will be able to say that these, in assisting the messengers, did what they did for Him. While one may conclude on the basis of a casual glance that these will be admitted into the kingdom on the basis of works, a closer examination will reveal that the faith principle will be operating. They will not be admitted because of their works, but, rather, their works will demonstrate their faith, which will be the basis for their admission into the kingdom. What will be involved is what James had in mind when he said, "What good is it, my brothers, if a man claims to have faith, but has no deeds? Can such faith save him? Suppose a brother or sister is without clothes and daily food. If one of you says to him, 'Go, I wish you well; keep warm and well fed,' but does nothing about his physical needs, what good is it? In the same way, faith by itself, if it is not accompanied by action, is dead" (James 2:14–17).

The King will then address those on his left and command, "Depart from me, you who are cursed, into the eternal fire prepared for the devil and his angels" (Matt. 25:41). Thus those classified as goats will be excluded from the King's kingdom. The King will explain, "I was hungry and you gave me nothing to eat, I was thirsty and you gave me nothing to drink, I was a stranger and you did not invite me in, I needed clothes and you did not clothe me, I was sick and in prison and you did not look after me"

(vv. 42–43). The condemned will claim that such a sentence is unjust because they never had an opportunity to do these things for Christ. However, He will reply, "Whatever you did not do for one of the least of these [that is, Christ's brothers], you did not do for me" (v. 45). These, like those who were classified as sheep, had heard the message of the messengers; yet out of fear of the wrath of the Beast, they had refused to assist the messengers, thereby showing that they had rejected the message of the messengers. By their lack of works they had demonstrated their lack of faith, and so the King will say, "They will go away to eternal punishment, but the righteous to eternal life" (v. 46).

In this parable Christ was showing that, following the judgment of living Israelites, He as King will pass judgment on living Gentiles. Those who have demonstrated their faith by their works will be accepted into His kingdom, and those who demonstrate their lack of faith by their lack of works will be excluded from His earthly, millennial kingdom. No unsaved person, whether Jew or Gentile, will enter Messiah's messianic kingdom. The kingdom to be instituted will be composed of those who have received the salvation that was provided by the King during His first advent here on the earth.

AN INTERPRETATION OF THE DOCTRINE OF THE KINGDOM IN THE PARABLES

In response to the disciples' question, "Why do you speak to the people in parables?" (Matt. 13:10), Christ replied, "The knowledge of the secrets of the kingdom of heaven has been given to you" (v. 11). Christ thus made it clear that the parables were designed to reveal truth concerning the theocratic kingdom program of God. Christ introduced His parables many times with the formula, "The kingdom of heaven is like" (13:24, 31, 33, 44–45, 47; 18:23; 20:1, 22:2; 25:1). Using the individual parables, Christ revealed various facets of truth concerning the theocratic kingdom. It will prove beneficial to arrange the parables thematically so as to develop a doctrine of the kingdom based on this portion of Christ's teaching.

THE OFFER OF THE KINGDOM

The uniqueness of Christ's offer

Because of the covenants and promises of the prophets, the nation of Israel was anticipating a kingdom over which David's son would rule. They expected a literal kingdom containing literal people. However, because of their indoctrination by the Pharisees, they had come to believe that they were in the kingdom. Christ spoke the parables of the patched garment and the wineskins (Luke 5:36–39) in order to show that He had not come to build on Pharisaism. He would not fulfill the covenant by perpetuating the doctrine of the Pharisees; rather, He had come to introduce a kingdom that was new and unique and had no relationship to the concepts of the kingdom currently accepted.

Christ the Good Shepherd

Because His right to assume the messianic role was rejected and His claims debated, Christ spoke the parable of the shepherd and his sheep (John 10:1–18). He wanted to prove that since He

161

had come in the way the prophets had predicted, He was truly the Messiah. He then revealed that those who are truly His, and consequently are a part of His kingdom, would recognize Him even though the nation rejected Him. He would lead His own out of the bondage of Pharisaism and bring them into the liberty that characterized His kingdom.

The welcome extended to sinners to enter the kingdom

The Pharisees had a perverted and distorted concept of the character of God. Recognizing that God is holy, they concluded that He could not and would not receive sinners into His kingdom. They reasoned that one's goal in life should be to produce enough righteous works to gain admission into the kingdom. They taught that God hated sinners and rejoiced in a sinner's death because then the sinner was removed from His presence forever.

In order to correct this wrong teaching our Lord taught the three parables of the searching shepherd, the searching housewife, and the welcoming father (Luke 15:1–32). In the parables of the lost sheep and the lost coin, Jesus put the emphasis on the diligent search conducted by the owners until what was lost had been found, and then He stressed the joy that came to the owners when what was lost was restored to them. In the third parable our Lord emphasized the heart of the father. Even though there was no worthiness in the son, the father eagerly awaited the son's return and had prepared a robe, ring, and sandals to confer authority on the son. In addition, the father had prepared a banquet through which he revealed his joy at his son's return. Christ told these parables, then, to emphasize that any sinner is welcome to avail himself of the offer that He was making and to enter into the kingdom in the way that He as the Messiah had prescribed.

Warning against rejection

The people in the nation looked to the Pharisees for leadership in religious matters. The Pharisees were considered as shepherds, and the people felt obligated to follow their lead. In the parable of the blind man leading a blind man (Luke 6:39), Christ was warning against following the Pharisees, who already had indicated their intent to reject Him. If the people followed their leaders, they would be destroyed, for the leaders themselves were spiritually blind. This parable, then, recognized the possibility of the nation's rejection since He already had been rejected by the leaders.

The announcement of the kingdom

In the parable of a king who prepared a wedding banquet for his son (Matt. 22:1–14), Christ indicated that an invitation was being given to that generation to enter the covenanted kingdom. The original announcement had been sent to the friends of the bridegroom at the time of the betrothal. Then some twelve months passed and the marriage was ready to be completed. According to the custom, a second invitation was now extended to those invited at the time of the betrothal in order that they might attend the wedding banquet and share the bridegroom's joy. The fact that a second invitation was being announced shows that the wedding was at hand. Since Christ was using the wedding banquet as a figure for His millennial kingdom, we know this parable teaches the offer of the kingdom. However, not all who were invited chose to attend; hence the invitation was extended a second time and even a third time in order that the banquet hall might be filled with guests. It is clear that the covenanted and prophesied kingdom was being offered to that generation. Jesus taught the same truth in the parable of the man who was preparing a great banquet (Luke 14:16–24), where the guests also had received a previous announcement and later were told that the banquet was ready and that they were invited to come.

Invitation in the light of the offer of the kingdom

In the light of the offer, Christ extended the following invitation: "Enter through the narrow gate. For wide is the gate and broad is the road that leads to destruction, and many enter through it. But small is the gate and narrow the road that leads to life, and only a few find it" (Matt. 7:13–14). Christ then gave a warning that revealed the danger of neglecting the invitation He had just given. In the parable of the wise and foolish builders (vv. 24–27), Christ likened His words to a rock on which a person may build. A house built on such a secure foundation will stand through every storm. Christ likened the teaching of the Pharisees to sand. If a person builds on this foundation, the structure will collapse when a storm comes. The nation was faced with a decision. On the one hand, they could accept Christ's words and enter the kingdom through trusting in Him. If, on the other hand, they rejected His words and accepted the doctrine of the Pharisees, they would be excluded from the kingdom. Thus the invitation to enter the kingdom was coupled with a warning not to try to enter the kingdom any other way than through Christ Himself.

THE REJECTION OF THE OFFER

In a number of His parables Christ indicated that the nation would reject His offer. Thus in the parable of the physician who was called on to heal himself (Luke 4:23), Christ perceived the unbelief of the nation. They would ask Him to prove that He was the Messiah since He so claimed to be. No one would consult a physician who could not heal. The inference was that Christ was a sinner; before He could offer salvation as a prerequisite for entrance into the kingdom, He needed to deal effectively with His own sins.

The parable of the wedding banquet (Matt. 22:1–14) not only emphasized the offer of the kingdom, but revealed the response of the invited guests to the invitation that had been extended to them. The guests were occupied with personal pursuits and refused to be interrupted in order to respond to the invitation. In like manner in the parable of the great banquet (Luke 14:16–24), the invited guests "began to make excuses" (v. 18). In these parables invitations had been extended and received; the recipients considered their response and chose to ignore the banquet to which they had been invited.

The rejection of the kingdom was further revealed in the parable of the landowner who planted a vineyard (Matt. 21:33–44). The landowner, anticipating the harvest of his vineyard, sent servants to collect the fruit. However, the tenants beat, stoned, and killed the servants. This part of the parable revealed the attitude of the nation in times past toward the prophets, who exhorted the people to repentance in view of the promise of the Davidic kingdom. The landowner finally sent his son to claim the harvest, but the tenants killed him. Again, this reveals the response of the nation to the kingdom offer that Messiah was making.

THE POSTPONEMENT OF THE KINGDOM

The Davidic covenant was to be the fulfillment of the unconditional, eternal covenants that God gave to the nation of Israel. In His covenant promises to Abraham (Gen. 12:1–3; 13:14–17; 15:18–20; 17:4–8), God said that Abraham's physical descendants would inhabit the land that God had deeded to Abraham permanently. In the covenant with David (2 Sam. 7:16), God promised that a descendant of David would sit on David's throne and rule over his house. This covenanted program was offered to Israel but was rejected by the nation. Because the covenants are eternal, unconditional, and therefore irrevocable, the Davidic kingdom program could not be canceled. It could, however, be postponed. Christ spoke the parable of the ten minas (Luke 19:11–27) in order to teach that the kingdom offer was being withdrawn and the Davidic form of the theocracy postponed. The Lord told of a nobleman who "went to a distant country to have himself appointed king and then to return" (v. 12). Because the man was of noble birth, he had the right to rule. His absence from his realm did not abrogate his right. When he returned from his journey, he would exercise the rights that belonged to him. In this manner Christ was affirming that Israel's rejection of Him as Messiah did not set aside His rights, nor did His absence mean that He had relinquished His rights. In His own time He would return to exercise the reign that is rightly His.

Christ inferred this same fact in the parable of the watchman at the door (Mark 13:34–37). Christ spoke of the owner of a household who was leaving his domain for an extended absence. This portion of the parable emphasized Christ's postponement of the kingdom and His absence from the realm in which the kingdom would be instituted at His return.

Christ further taught this truth in the parable of the landowner who planted a vineyard (Matt. 21:33–44). Because the tenants produced no fruit to give to the landowner, he decided to take the vineyard from them and give it to other tenants. Christ interpreted this portion of the parable, saying, "The kingdom of God will be taken away from you and given to a people who will produce its fruit" (v. 43). The main teaching is the same despite a difference of opinion among expositors on the detail of whether the people to whom the kingdom will be given be the Gentiles through whom God will work in the present age, or a future generation in the nation of Israel to whom the kingdom will be reoffered during the Tribulation. Christ's central teaching was that the kingdom would be removed and postponed until a future time.

THE JUDGMENT ON THAT GENERATION BECAUSE OF THEIR REJECTION OF THE MESSIAH

In a number of parables Christ spoke of the judgment that would fall on that generation because of their rejection of Him. In the parable of the landowner who planted the vineyard (Matt. 21:33–34), Christ had pictured Himself as the stone that the builders rejected (v. 42) and then He had announced that "on whom it [the stone] falls will be crushed" (v. 44). Christ thus pictured Himself as a Judge who would mete out judgment to the guilty. In the parable of the cleansed household (Matt. 12:43–45), Christ depicted the nation as having undergone a cleansing through the ministry of John the Baptist. However, that cleansing was not permanent. The unclean spirit that had left the house took seven other spirits that were more wicked than itself, and they entered and occupied the house that had been cleansed.

Christ stated, "The final condition of that man is worse than the first" (v. 45). By this He indicated that the state of the nation was lower as a consequence of their rejection of Him than it had been before John began his ministry of calling the nation to repentance. Christ said, "That is how it will be with this wicked generation" (v. 45). Christ meant that just as the man's condition was worse at the end than at the beginning, so the same was true of Israel. This parable shows that while an offer had been made that, if accepted, would have removed judgment, the nation had rejected the offer and so judgment must come.

THE NEW FORM OF THE KINGDOM

The promised and Davidic form of the theocracy offered to that generation by Jesus Christ was rejected. He therefore passed judgment on that generation, and the offer of the Davidic kingdom was withdrawn. However, because the kingdom was based on an eternal unconditional covenant, it could not be abrogated; instead, it was postponed to some indeterminate future time. Christ chose to reveal through parables the form of the theocracy through which God would evidence His sovereign authority during this present age. As noted earlier the parables were designed to reveal truth to believers and to hide truth from the unbelievers (cf. "Christ's Use of Parables" in INTRODUCTION). Many of the parables revealing the course of this present age are recorded in Matthew 13. Without doubt, Christ repeated the parables to instruct the disciples concerning the course of this present age on many different occasions. The parables in Matthew 13 reveal a number of significant characteristics of the kingdom in the present age. In the parable of the sower, the seed, and the soils (Matt. 13:3–23) Christ revealed that this age will be characterized by a sowing of seed that He interpreted as the "word of God" (Luke 8:12), by a Sower who is Himself, followed by a sowing by those whom He would appoint to this ministry. The sowing would be done throughout the world. No longer would Israel be the primary recipient of the message as was true in the Old Testament and during the ministry of the apostles in the

Gospels and early chapters of Acts. To this sowing there would be varied responses, depending on the attitude of the hearers. Thus the world-wide dissemination of the truth that Christ revealed would be the first characteristic of the age.

Christ revealed another significant characteristic through the parable of the weeds (Matt. 13:24–30). In this parable He disclosed that Satan will try to defeat the program of God and exercise his right to rule by sowing weeds among the good seed that the Sower has sowed. Satan has always opposed God's right to rule and has sought to exercise dominion himself. In this new form of the kingdom, Satan will actively seek to prevent the exercise of God's sovereign authority. Since Satan is an imitator, the weeds that he sows bear a striking resemblance to wheat. It is not possible until the time of harvest to distinguish between the wheat and weeds. Wheat can be identified by the grain it produces; the weeds (perhaps darnel) produce no usable grain. Thus one involved in the kingdom program in the present age may anticipate the opposition of Satan in doing the Lord's work.

The previous parables have dealt with the outward development of the kingdom. Now in two parables Christ dealt with the internal characteristics of the kingdom.

In the parable of the seed growing by itself (Mark 4:26–29), Christ called attention to how physical seed germinates and grows because of the essential life in the seed. Similarly, Christ said, when the new form of the kingdom is introduced by the sowing of the seed of God's Word, that kingdom will develop by the power in the seed that was sown. Just as a sower's work is completed when physical seed is put into the soil, so human responsibility will end when the message has been proclaimed. In the unfolding of the kingdom program, the development of the kingdom will not depend on human agency but on the power of the Word that has been proclaimed.

In the parable of the mustard seed, Christ revealed that the kingdom would begin with an insignificant beginning but grow to great proportions. The mustard plant is an annual that can grow to tree size in one season. Thus it can be a place of refuge for the birds that perch in its branches. Christ's emphasis here was to contrast the size of the mustard seed and the plant that came forth from that seed. The new form of the kingdom began essentially with eleven men. From that insignificant beginning it grew so extensively that one could say when the Book of Acts closed that the whole world had heard the gospel (cf. Rom. 1:8; Col. 1:6).

In the parable of the yeast mixed into a large amount of flour, Christ revealed that when the new form of the kingdom began, it would work irreversibly, persistently, and pervasively throughout this present age. Just as yeast introduced into flour continues to work until the mixture is ready for baking in an oven, so when the kingdom message was introduced, it would work continuously throughout the age.

In the parables of the hidden treasure and the pearl, Christ revealed God's purpose for the kingdom in this present age. His emphasis was on the value of the treasure and pearl that purchasers obtained through great personal sacrifice. By His death Christ was to become a propitiation for the sins of the world (1 John 2:2). As a result of Christ's propitiatory act, the world was reconciled to God (2 Cor. 5:18–19). God's plan in the present age is to acquire for Himself a treasure. Since the field or the land is a frequent reference in Scripture to Israel, the parable of the treasure hidden in the field may emphasize that God will receive to Himself some from among that nation during this present age (Rom. 11:5). Since the pearl comes out of the sea and the sea is used in Scripture to represent Gentile nations (cf. Isa. 57:20), the second parable may emphasize that God will call to Himself many from among the Gentile peoples as His own possession. This is the basis of Paul's doctrine of the nature of the church in Ephesians 2:11–22.

The parable of the net reveals that at the end of this age a judgment will separate the good from the bad, and the useful from the useless, in the same way a fisherman divides his catch. Prior to the establishment of the millennial kingdom, there will be a judgment to exclude the unsaved and to invite the saved to participate in the joys and blessings of Christ's reign. In the parable of the householder (Matt. 13:52), Christ likened Himself to the custodian of a storehouse who brings forth the items that will meet the needs of the household. The custodian may bring forth old grain or new grain, or old wine or new wine. But through what he brings forth, he fully meets the needs of the household. Christ was revealing in these parables concerning the new form of the kingdom that some aspects of this new form would be like previous forms of the kingdom; on the other hand, some aspects would be entirely new. The fact that there would be a kingdom was revealed in the Old Testament, but an aspect that was new was that it would be proclaimed throughout the world. The kingdom in the Old Testament was for Israel, even though Gentiles were to be blessed in the kingdom. However, a new truth was that Jews and Gentiles would participate equally in this new form of the kingdom. Thus in the new form of the kingdom, we do find some features that are similar to the old, but we also discover other features that are unique to the new.

EXHORTATIONS IN VIEW OF THE COMING OF CHRIST TO ESTABLISH THE MILLENNIAL KINGDOM

In response to the disciples' question concerning the signs that would forewarn of the end of the age and the coming of Christ, the Lord enumerated many signs (Matt. 24:4–26) that would find fulfillment in the seven years of the Tribulation. These signs will be given to alert a disobedient people to whom the kingdom is being offered again (v. 14) of the approach of the Judge. To stress the importance of these signs, Christ spoke the parable of the fig tree (vv. 32–35). Just as the first new shoots on a fig tree, or any tree (Luke 21:29), indicate the arrival of spring and herald the advent of summer, so the appearance of these signs will warn the nation of Israel of the momentous event that they forecast, that is, the return of Messiah.

The response that these signs were designed to produce is revealed in several brief parables. In the parable of the doorkeeper (Mark 13:33–37), Christ emphasized that the servant assigned to keep watch at the door is to be faithful to this assignment because the servant does not know just when the master will return. It is incumbent on that servant to diligently watch without interruption. Thus in this parable Christ emphasized faithfulness in the light of the unexpectedness of His return.

In the parable of the watchful owner (Matt. 24:42–44), Christ again emphasized watchfulness and preparedness. If a thief served notice when he would arrive to plunder a home, the owner would not need to secure his household until the appointed hour arrived. However, since a thief gives no notice, a theft could occur at any time; and the owner of the house must keep the household secured. By this parable Christ emphasized the necesssity of being prepared and being faithful in view of the unexpectedness of Messiah's return.

In the parable of the wise and wicked servants (Matt. 24:45–51), Christ emphasized the need for faithfulness to the assigned responsibilities in view of the approach of the Lord's return as indicated in the signs. A wise servant will fulfill assigned responsibilities, but a foolish servant will neglect assigned duties and live to indulge the flesh. Such a faithless servant will be deprived of the joys of the kingdom when the master returns. Thus in these brief parables Christ gave exhortations to watchfulness, preparedness, and faithfulness in view of His return as indicated in the signs that will be given.

EVENTS PREPARING FOR THE ESTABLISHMENT OF THE MILLENNIAL KINGDOM

In the parables revealing the characteristics of the present age, Christ revealed that this age will end in judgment. However, no details were given at that time. In the lengthy parables in Matthew 25, Christ did reveal details concerning this judgment program.

Judgment on living Israel

Following Christ's second advent to the earth (Matt. 24:30), angels will regather living Israel from the four corners of the earth where they had been scattered during the Tribulation (v. 31). These will be brought back into the land given by covenant to

Abraham (Gen. 12:7). The Old Testament made it clear that repentance and restoration to fellowship with the God against whom the Israelites had sinned was a prerequisite for the enjoyment of the covenanted kingdom blessings (Deut. 30:1–10). Thus it was revealed that no unsaved person would enter the promised kingdom. This judgment on living Israel is described in the parable of the wise and foolish virgins (Matt. 25:1–13). Immediately preceding this parable, Christ had exhorted His hearers to be watchful, faithful, and prepared. This parable of the wise and foolish virgins reveals that there will be a judgment to determine the preparedness of those in Israel alive at the time of the Second Advent. The virgins in the Oriental wedding refer to the guests at the banquet who are contrasted with the bride who appears with the bridegroom. The invitation had been extended to the nation to prepare themselves to enter the millennial kingdom, which could be expected imminently (Matt. 24:14). The nation was now assembled and was expecting to enjoy the wedding banquet, which is the Lord's figure for the Davidic, millennial kingdom. When the announcement was made that the bridegroom was approaching, the assembled guests lit their lamps in order that they might meet him. The wise were prepared for the bridegroom's return and had brought supplemental oil to replenish their lamps. The foolish had made no preparation, and so they were unprepared when the bridegroom returned. The prepared guests were accepted into the millennial banquet. The unprepared guests sought to prepare themselves, but found that the door to the banquet hall was shut; and they were denied admission. Thus in this parable Christ taught that living Israel would be brought back to the land for a judgment to determine who was prepared and who was unprepared. Those who are prepared will be accepted into the Messiah's millennial kingdom, but the unprepared will be excluded.

Judgment on living Gentiles

In the parable of the sheep and goats (Matt. 25:31–46), Christ revealed that Gentiles will be gathered to judgment. They will be divided into two groups. Those classified as sheep will be accepted into the kingdom, but those called goats will be excluded from it. The sheep will be received because of what they did for Christ. In response to the surprise registered by those on His right hand, Christ explained that the treatment afforded His brothers was done for Him. The term "brothers" (Matt. 25:40) seems to have reference to either the nation of Israel as a whole, or the chosen ones from among Israel (Rev. 7) who will proclaim the gospel during the Tribulation. These will not be accepted because of their works, for no man is saved by works; rather, their works will prove the genuineness of their faith. Having demonstrated a faith validated by works, they will be accepted into the kingdom. Conversely, those on the left will not have produced works, and this lack will reveal the absence of faith. Because those on the left have no faith, they will be excluded from the kingdom. In this parable Christ explained the tests to be given the Gentiles to prove the state of their preparedness as individuals. Those on the right will be accepted into the kingdom, but those on the left will be excluded from the kingdom. Thus in these two judgments the whole world will be brought to judgment in preparation for the establishment of the millennial kingdom.

Judgment for reward

In the parable of the talents (Matt. 25:14–30), Christ revealed that there will be a judgment prior to the millennial kingdom to test one's faithfulness. Responsibilities were assigned by a master to his servants for which they were held accountable. At the master's return the servants were called to account. Those found faithful were admitted into the master's domain and given positions of responsibility in the administration of his affairs. On the other hand, one servant was found unfaithful and was cast out of the household and excluded from any responsibility in the master's domain.

Christ in this parable revealed that not only one's preparedness but also one's faithfulness will be tested. The unfaithful will reveal their lack of faith by their unfaithfulness and will be excluded from the kingdom. By their faithfulness others will reveal the existence of their faith, and they will not only be received into the kingdom but will be given responsibilities to be exercised in the kingdom age to come.

These judgments, then, will be preparatory to the institution of the millennial kingdom. The wicked will be excluded from the kingdom, and the righteous will be received into it. Judgments were anticipated when Christ had just previously said, "Two men will be in the field; one will be taken [away in judgment] and the other left [to go into the kingdom]. Two women will be grinding with a hand mill; one will be taken [away in judgment] and the other left [to go into Messiah's kingdom]" (Matt. 24:40–41). There will also be a judgment to distribute rewards for the faithful that will be enjoyed during the Messiah's millennial reign.

LIFE IN THE KINGDOM

The parables thus far have dealt with the kingdom program. In them Christ taught concerning the offer of the kingdom, the judgment on that generation because of the kingdom, and the new form of the kingdom. Christ gave exhortations in view of the coming of the King and outlined events preceding the establishment of the Davidic form of the theocracy.

Many parables were directed to the disciples to instruct them concerning life in the kingdom. These parables reveal what the King expects of His subjects.

Obedience

In the parable of the two sons (Matt. 21:28–32), Christ taught that obedience is a test of sonship. This parable counteracted the popular teaching of the Pharisees that all of Abraham's physical descendants were already in the kingdom by virtue of their relationship to the patriarch. In the present parable Christ revealed that a person's right to enter the kingdom will be determined not by his profession but by his obedience to the King. Obedience will not only be a test of eligibility, but it will be required of those who are in the kingdom. They must be subject to the rule of the King.

Love

During the course of his earthly life, Christ had demonstrated the compassion of God toward the poor, the sick, the sorrowing, the outcast, and the sinful. Compassion such as He demonstrated will be required of those who are His subjects in the kingdom. In the parable of the two debtors (Luke 7:41–50), Christ taught the basis for love. This parable was spoken in the house of a Pharisee where a sinful woman lavished manifestations of her devotion on the person of Christ. The Pharisee could neither understand why the woman would love Him, nor why He would accept such evidences of her lavish devotion. In the parable Christ told of two debtors who had been forgiven, one a large debt, and the other a small debt. Christ asked the Pharisee who would love the forgiving creditor the most, and the obvious answer was that the one who had been forgiven most would love the most. Christ in this parable explained to the Pharisee why the woman loved Him. She was a notorious sinner who had been forgiven much. The parable also answered the Pharisee's question as to why Christ would accept her devotion. The answer was that her devotion arose out of the love that the experience of forgiveness had generated in her as a result of the forgiveness she had received.

From this parable, then, we learn that love for Christ will be shown by the one who has experienced His gracious forgiveness. Further, we see that Christ will accept that love when it flows from one who has received His forgiveness.

In the parable of the Good Samaritan (Luke 10:30–37), we discover that mercy that is a manifestation of love is to be demonstrated to anyone who is our neighbor. From the parable we learn that our neighbor is anyone in need, whose need we know and whose need we are able to meet. The fact that Christ commanded the scholar in the law to go and do as the Samaritan had done reveals that such mercy is a mark of those who are in the kingdom, for it is a fulfillment of the righteousness demanded by the law. The subjects of the King in the kingdom, then, must not only demonstrate love toward God, because of the forgiveness that has been received, but also love toward their neighbors.

Thus life in the kingdom must fulfill the requirements of the law, which said, "'Love the Lord with all your heart and with all your soul and with all your strength and with all your mind'; and, 'Love your neighbor as yourself'" (Luke 10:27). The two parables dealing with love, then, describe an important characteristic of life in the kingdom.

Prayer

Prayer is primarily an act of worship in which the one praying submits to the authority of the One to whom the prayer is offered. By prayer one registers total dependence on the One to whom the prayer is addressed. These facts concerning prayer suggest that it will play an important role in life in the kingdom.

The basis of prayer. In the parable of the Pharisee and the tax collector (Luke 18:9–14), Christ revealed the basis on which one may approach God in prayer. The Pharisee thought he could approach God on the basis of his works and so he reiterated in his prayer the evidences of his righteousness. However, these are repudiated as providing a basis on which one may address prayer to God.

On the other hand, the tax collector recognized that there was nothing in himself to commend himself to God. He gazed toward the ground and beat his breast in humiliation. By faith he put himself under the propitiating blood that was provided on the Day of Atonement and under which the unworthy could take refuge. Because he put himself under blood, Christ said he "went home justified before God" (Luke 18:14). Thus in this parable Christ gave instruction as to the basis on which people will approach God to offer worship, praise, thanksgiving, petition, and intercession in the kingdom.

Persistence in prayer. In several parables Christ taught the necessity of persisting in order to obtain an answer to prayer. In the parable of the persistent widow (Luke 18:1–8), Christ revealed that even a hard-hearted, indifferent judge can be moved by the persistence of a widow to grant her request. The judge was not moved by the justice of her claim, and he did not react emotionally to her need. He granted her request because of her persistence. In the parable of the persistent friend (Luke 11:5–13), Christ had stressed this same truth. Hospitality placed a responsibility on the host that he, because of the late hour, was not able to fulfill; however, the host knew one who could meet the need and asked for that friend's help. Because of the lateness of the hour, the friend refused to disturb the entire household in order to grant the request. But the host persisted until the need was met. The application that Christ drew was (using a literal translation of Luke 11:9): "Keep on asking and it will be given to you; keep on seeking and you will find; keep on knocking and the door will be opened to you. For everyone who keeps on asking receives; he who keeps on seeking finds; and to him who keeps on knocking, the door will be opened."

This parable provides a definition of intercessory prayer. The one who presented the request to the friend was not the one in need; rather, the petitioner was representing another who was in need. An intercessor, then, is a go-between who stands between one in need and the one who can meet the need. Intercessory prayer, then, is totally unselfish, for it is not concerned with petitions for oneself but rather for the needs of others. Thus unselfish intercessory prayer will be a characteristic of life in the kingdom.

The use of wealth

The Pharisees counted wealth as a certain sign of God's blessing. They strove to accumulate material possessions to assure themselves that they were righteous to a degree that rendered them acceptable to God. It became necessary for Christ to devote much teaching to correct this wrong attitude toward wealth. In telling parables about the use of wealth, Christ was revealing characteristics of life in the kingdom.

1. *The use of present opportunities.* In the parable of the shrewd manager (Luke 16:1–13), Christ stressed that a righteous person will not misuse a stewardship selfishly, thinking only of the present; instead, a righteous person will act wisely and with a

view to a future reckoning in the stewardship. Christ related that when the unfaithfulness of a manager caused the loss of his privileges, he wisely used the position he held, not for selfish indulgence in the present, but wisely with a view to the future. By reducing the indebtedness of his master's debtors, he won favor for himself. Christ did not approve of the manager's devious conduct, but He did commend the manager for wisdom in using present opportunities, not for the present only, but for the future.

Christ applied this principle to the use of wealth. He asked, "If you have not been trustworthy in handling worldly wealth, who will trust you with true riches?" (Luke 16:11). Thus Christ taught that a mark of life in the kingdom will be the wise use of material possessions.

2. *The temporary nature of material things.* In the parable of the rich man and the beggar (Luke 16:19–31), Christ taught that material wealth is not permanent but only temporary. The rich man who died left all his material possessions behind. The soul of the rich man continued to exist, but the end of his earthly life meant he no longer could use his material wealth. The parable further teaches that wealth is not a basis of salvation. No doubt the wealthy man was schooled in the Pharisaic doctrine that held out the hope that he was acceptable to God because he possessed wealth. The parable revealed that the poor beggar was accepted, not the wealthy man. This leads to the observation that a rich man, according to biblical concepts, is not one who has great material riches, but one who loves what God has given and trusts Him for salvation. The parable also reveals that, contrary to the Pharisaic concept, poverty is not necessarily an evidence of God's displeasure or punishment for sin. The beggar was not accepted into heaven because he was poor, but his poverty was no barrier to his entrance to true riches.

3. *The reward of covetousness.* The parable of the rich fool (Luke 12:16–21) shows that one's use of wealth will reveal whether one is righteous or unrighteous. The parable concerns a man, already wealthy, whose riches were greatly increased by an abundant harvest that his land produced. The extensive harvest

gave the man an opportunity to demonstrate that he fulfilled the righteousness of the law by distributing his wealth to his neighbors in need. However, he refused to do this and instead set the goods aside for his own use. By such a use of his wealth, the man showed he was unrighteous according to the demands of the law. Thus in the parable Christ was stressing that wealth must be rightly used during this life if it is to provide any benefits in the life to come.

Faithfulness

The parable of the faithful and wise manager (Luke 12:42–48) emphasizes that privilege brings responsibility and that responsibility entails accountability. If one is appointed to a position of authority and then misuses that authority, that one will forfeit the authority. When Paul taught, "It is required that those who have been given a trust must prove faithful" (1 Cor. 4:2), he reiterated the truth that Christ spoke in this parable. Faithfulness to privileges and responsibilities will be a characteristic of life in the kingdom.

Humility

In the parable concerning seats at the wedding feast (Luke 14:7–11), Christ warned against seeking preeminence for oneself. True honor is not what one confers on oneself but what others confer in recognition of worthiness. Therefore, Christ commanded that one is to take a lower seat as a sign of humility and let the host confer the honor on the one who deserves it.

In the Beatitudes (Matt. 5:3–12), Christ gave the characteristics of righteous people. From the features that characterize life in the kingdom as revealed in the parables, we observe that those characteristics required in the Beatitudes will be realized in those who are citizens of the kingdom.

Thus I develop a doctrine of the theocratic kingdom from the parables, tracing the offer by Christ, its rejection by Israel, its consequent postponement to a future time, the resultant judgment on the generation that rejected Christ's offer, the new form of the theocracy to be developed in the present age, the events preceding the establishment of the coming messianic kingdom as well as the characteristics of those who are in the kingdom. Well do we pray, "Come, Lord Jesus."